Strong Women Speak
on Leadership, Success
and Living Well

Lessons for Life from Strong Women
Through the Ages

Adriana Fuentes Díaz
Steven Howard

Caliente Press

Strong Women Speak on Leadership, Success and Living Well

Lessons for Life from Strong Women Through the Ages

ISBN: 978-1-943702-38-1 (Print edition)
   978-1-943702-39-8 (Kindle edition)

Published by:
Caliente Press
1775 E Palm Canyon Drive, Suite 110-198
Palm Springs, CA 92264
U.S.A.
Email: steven@CalientePress.com

Cover Illustration: Berenice Lacroix
Cover Design: Héctor Castañeda

ENDORSEMENTS AND PRAISE

I'm reading and I love it! It seems incredible to me how this type of reading can be inspiring for many people.

The idea of teaching about leadership seems fabulous to share it through this book. It motivates us to always keep going, grow as human beings, and discover saved skills.

Sometimes we are not aware of the power that we have that inspired women like you knock on our door showing us infinite possibilities for enrichment, empowerment, and transformation.

With all my love to my great friend Adriana and Steven, wishing you all the success in the world!

Oriana Fabricatore
Preschool Teacher
Venezuela and Spain

I am recommending this book because my wonderful friend Adriana and Steven are helping to transform and empower women achieve success. Not only do they live these values, but now they share their inner light, inspiration, and wisdom.

I think is a beautiful book to give to your mom, best friends, sister, cousin, or mother-in-law because it has a powerful message of self-love and giving back. I cannot wait to share this book with my daughter Sofia.

Ana María Barreneche
X-Ray Tech Specialist
USA

Strong Women Speak on Leadership, Success and Living Well: Lessons for Life from Strong Women Through the Ages is a beautiful gift one can make for herself or another woman as a sign of love, appreciation, and support.

I would love to see this book within an arm's-length reach of as many women as possible so that we can always open it and lean into the wisdom of others around us. Whether you feel sad, discouraged, tired, afraid, lost, or frustrated, on these pages you will always find words that will help you feel supported and understood, and help you keep going. Each of us is a strong human, so let us link arms and make this world a better place, just as the women on these pages are teaching us.

Anna Liebel
Leadership Consultant
Iceland

An inspiring book, which gave me the sensation of learning from many stories where each one concentrates a great teaching.

Reading each sentence is comforting and invites you to reflect. It is the sum of many points of view that nurture raising knowledge, because each day is a new opportunity to grow. Adriana and Steven have captured through their research a compilation of phrases that resonate and have given me a wonderful time by being inspired by them while reading them.

Thank you, thank you, thank you for this wonderful contribution.

Enrique Núñez García
Senior Executive, Audiovisual Industry
Venezuela and México

I absolutely loved this book! I will put it on my breakfast table to just flip open every morning to let these words inspire me. As an entrepreneur having guiding lights out there is essential and the collection here is phenomenal.

Lena Rekdal
Founder of Nimmersion AB
Sweden

There is a wonderful purpose behind this book. A very inspiring and single-minded collection of strong, successful, and challenging woman thoughts and life lessons. Deep reflections from the authors to set-up each section that fully engage the reader and transform its perspective to a more human, close, and assertive leadership style in both life and business fields.

Alfonso Alcocer
VP Business Director, BBDO
México

Leaders use words to fuel passion, resolve, commitment, and action. In *Strong Women Speak on Leadership, Success and Living Well* you will find leadership quotes from powerful women that can be used as daily shots of inspiration to drive your own resolve and passion.

Seeing how women have used words to help guide and influence others demonstrates leadership possibilities for us all.

Holly Burkett, PhD
Award-winning Author
Learning for the Long Run: 7 Practices for Sustaining a
Learning Organization
USA

Contents

Dedication

We dedicate this book to all the strong women breaking gender barriers, crashing through glass ceilings, battling on the frontline against the coronavirus, and destroying the myth that women are a weaker sex.

And to the women who are helping other women build strong communities, families, businesses, support networks, societies, and futures.

This book is also dedicated to the current and future generations of women who will continue to remove from society the negative stereotypes that divide us through their actions, words, behaviors, mindsets, examples, and teachings.

Remember that all women have a purpose in life, and it is never too late to discover yours and pursue it. Always look for your inner strength to make all your dreams come true and, most importantly, believe in yourself and bet everything to be happy.

It is important to have strong images
of women out there,
women who aren't afraid of expressing themselves,
women who aren't afraid of taking chances,
women who aren't afraid of their own power.

Gina Torres

The purpose of our lives is to give birth
to the best which is within us.

Marianne Williamson

Introduction

Words inspire. Motivate. Inform. Educate. Console.

Great quotes prompt reflection, spark action. They often lead to new ideas, new memorable phrases, even new personal credos.

This is our goal with *Strong Women Speak on Leadership, Success and Living Well*. We want to inspire you. And have you use these words of wisdom from strong women through the ages motivate, inform, educate, and inspire you. You will leave your mark on this world by how you help others identify and develop their talents. This is a fundamental role of all leaders and a critical role for successful women to apply to other women.

When the pandemic hit in April 2020, the two of us sat down and drew up a list of projects that we could work on, either individually or together. Supporting one another on these projects — as well as on the many hurdles life has thrown at us — is the foundation of our strong relationship In Spanish, the phrase *más fuertes juntos* means we are stronger together. That is certainly the case for us.

This book culminates the trilogy we set out to create. Our goal has been to use the words of strong women from around the world to encourage and motivate the current and future generations of women.

The first two books in this trilogy – *When Strong Women Speak, Strong Women Listen* and *Strong Women Have Beliefs and Values* – were written by Adriana, with Steven as her editing and publishing coach. We are proud to have jointly written this book together.

One of Adriana's passions is to encourage successful women to help the growth and development of other women across the globe. Steven has a passion for developing young managers and leaders into great leaders. These two passions naturally synchronized into *Strong Women Speak on Leadership, Success and Living Well*.

The great tragedy of the human experience is not that there are evil people in the world doing terrible and selfish things. Rather, the biggest tragedy is that the majority of people live an existence that is far removed from their greatest possible intensity and passion levels. Their lives are lived mostly to satisfy the plans and desires of others, and they commonly feel that they have insufficient control over their respective life journeys.

A purposeful, self-determined, meaningful life can be lived. It takes continuous self-examination, introspection, a chosen path, determination, self-motivation, and a willingness to accept personal responsibility for the outcomes resulting from your actions, thoughts, behaviors, and emotions. But it can be done.

And remember, it is never too late to change your life and start over. To discover your inner strength and always believe in yourself. No one has or will have control of your life; only you. Always use it to improve, learn, love, laugh, dance, and be happy.

We hope that *Strong Women Speak on Leadership, Success and Living Well*, as well as the other two books in this *Strong Women Speak* series, will be influences that put and keep you on a life journey of passion, meaning, success, happiness, and wellbeing.

We hope you will take time to reflect upon the wise words and thoughts in this book from strong women who made a difference in the world. We also hope the ideas found within this book will provide inspiration and motivation for your personal growth and development.

Enjoy. Live life to its fullest. Help others whenever you can. And let's all leave the world a better place for our children and grandchildren.

Adriana Fuentes Díaz
Steven Howard
March 2021

CHAPTER 1

Leadership

Adriana

Leadership is the art of inspiring and leading a group of people. To be a leader you need the support of your followers and it is they who, noticing the skills and attitudes of a leader, choose that leader to guide them.

A leader is a person who directs, creates, promotes, motivates, and summons people in any type of situation to achieve goals.

Leadership can emerge naturally. When a person stands out in the role of leader, without the need to possess a position or a position that empowers him as such, that person is a true leader.

Today, leadership is considered a behavior that can be exercised and perfected. The skills of a leader involve charisma, patience, respect, integrity, knowledge, intelligence, discipline and, above all, the ability to positively influence others.

Steven

The concept of leadership has evolved over the years.

I believe great leadership is an art. It is the art of achieving progress through the involvement and actions of others.

This is why great leaders are strong in both leading people and leading for results, while good leaders typically focus their leadership on only one or the other.

Great leadership is not confined to the executive suites or ownership ranks. Great leaders can be found at all levels of an organization. And anyone, including you, can become a great leader!

Being power is like being a lady.
If you have to tell people you are, you aren't.
Margaret Thatcher

Leadership Quotes

Do what you feel in your heart to be right – for you'll be criticized anyway. You'll be damned if you do, and damned if you don't.
Eleanor Roosevelt

Today a reader, tomorrow a leader.
Margaret Fuller

Do not wait for leaders. Do it alone, person to person.
Mother Teresa

The supreme quality for leadership is unquestionably integrity. Without it, no real success is possible, no matter whether it is on a section gang, a football field, in an army or in an office.
Lucille Ball

You manage things; you lead people.
Rear Admiral Grace Murray Hopper

Leadership is about making others better as a result of your presence and making sure that impact lasts in your absence.
Sheryl Sandberg

Authority without wisdom is like a heavy axe without an edge, fitter to bruise than polish.
Anne Dudley Bradstreet

Some attributes of leadership are universal and are often about finding ways of encouraging people to combine their efforts, their talents, their insights, their enthusiasm, and their inspiration to work together.
Queen Elizabeth II

Power isn't control at all — power is strength, and giving that strength to others. A leader isn't someone who forces others to make him stronger; a leader is someone willing to give his strength to others that they may have the strength to stand on their own.
Beth Revis

A leader takes people where they want to go. A great leader takes people where they don't necessarily want to go, but ought to be.
Rosalynn Carter

Leadership is about making others better as a result of your presence and making sure that impact lasts in your absence.
Sheryl Sandberg

The most common way people give up their power is by thinking they don't have any.
Alice Walker

Leadership should be more participative than directive, more enabling than performing.
Mary D. Poole

As you enter positions of trust and power, dream a little before you think.
Toni Morrison

Being powerful is like being a lady. If you have to tell people you are, you aren't.
Margaret Thatcher

Responsibility equals accountability equals ownership. And a sense of ownership is the most powerful weapon a team or organization can have.
Pat Summitt

People who are truly strong lift others up. People who are truly powerful bring others together.
Michelle Obama

I never thought of myself as a woman leader or Latina leader; I just thought of myself as a leader.
Geisha Williams

Opportunities for leadership are all around us. The capacity for leadership is deep within us.
Madeleine Albright

I have also worked with leaders who have a positive outlook, and the morale is so different. Even when faced with challenges, the people looked for solutions.
Catherine Pulsifer

Leadership is not about men in suits. It is a way of life for those who know who they are and willing to be their best to create the life they want to live.
Kathleen Schafer

I am endlessly fascinated that playing football is considered a training ground for leadership, but raising children isn't.
Dee Dee Myers

The ability to learn is the most important quality a leader can have.
Sheryl Sandberg

Authenticity requires a certain measure of vulnerability, transparency, and integrity.
Janet Louise Stephenson

The important work of moving the world forward does not wait to be done by perfect men.
Mary Ann Evans

A leader is someone who is self-directed and does not allow anyone to place barriers.
Paulette Brown

Leadership is the ability to see a problem and then seek a solution and ACT — without sitting back and hoping and waiting for someone else to tackle it.
Evangeline Mitchell

Leaders can change the world if they are willing to take a courageous stand.
Saran Crayton

I wish you power that equals your intelligence and your strength. I wish you success that equals your talent and determination. And I wish you faith.
Betty Shabazz

If I'm not leading by example, then I'm not doing the right thing. And I want to always do the right thing.
Pat Summitt

Good leaders organize and align people around what the team needs to do. Great leaders motivate and inspire people with why they're doing it. That's purpose. And that's the key to achieving something truly transformational.
Marilyn Hewson

Leadership is not bullying and leadership is not aggression. Leadership is the expectation that you can use your voice for good. That you can make the world a better place.
Sheryl Sandberg

If you want to improve the organization, you have to improve yourself and the organization gets pulled up with you.
Indra Nooyi

Where there is no accountability, there will also be no responsibility.
Sunday Adelaja

When I dare to be powerful, to use my strength in the service of my vision, then it becomes less and less important whether I am afraid.
Audre Lorde

The power to command frequently causes failure to think.
Barbara Tuchman

The quality of strength lined with tenderness is an unbeatable combination.
Maya Angelou

Leadership is the ability to guide others without force into a direction or decision that leaves them still feeling empowered and accomplished.
Lisa Cash Hanson

True leadership stems from individuality that is honestly and sometimes imperfectly expressed. Leaders should strive for authenticity over perfection.
Sheryl Sandberg

The leadership instinct you are born with is the backbone. You develop the funny bone and the wishbone that go with it.
Elaine Agather

If leadership serves only the leader, it will fail. Ego satisfaction, financial gain, and status can all be valuable tools for a leader, but if they become the only motivations, they will eventually destroy a leader. Only when service for a common good is the primary purpose are you truly leading.
Sheila Murray Bethel

Our society needs women to be more numerous in decision-making positions and in entrepreneurial areas. We always have to pass a twofold test: first to prove that, though women, we are no idiots, and second, the test anybody has to pass.
Cristina Fernández de Kirchner

If you are a woman and you're assertive and you want to get the job done, you're a bitch. If you're a guy, you're just assertive.
Christina Aguilera

Your job as leader is to stay as close in touch as possible with those closest to the action.
Kat Cole

If you look confident you can pull off anything — even if you have no clue what you're doing.
Jessica Alba

I just love bossy women. I could be around them all day. To me, bossy is not a pejorative term at all. It means somebody's passionate and engaged and ambitious and doesn't mind learning.
Amy Poehler

The leader is the person who brings a little magic to the moment.
Denise Morrison

If more women are in leadership roles, we'll stop assuming they shouldn't be.
Sheryl Sandberg

I measure my own success as a leader by how well the people who work for me succeed.
Maria Shi

Leadership is about making others better as a result of your presence and making sure that impact lasts in your absence.
Sheryl Sandberg

I'd like to see a world where there are so many Latina women leaders — and women of all different backgrounds — in the top jobs around the country. When that happens, we've succeeded.
Geisha Williams

Don't mistake politeness for lack of strength.
Sonia Sotomayor

The goal of many leaders is to get people to think more highly of the leader. The goal of a great leader is to help people think more highly of themselves.
J. Carla Northcutt

Good leadership requires you to surround yourself with people of diverse perspectives who can disagree with you without fear of retaliation.
Doris Kearns Goodwin

Every political leader worth their salt in history — from Gandhi to Martin Luther King — has expressed the same message, which is courage. Real leaders don't tell people to be frightened. They help people find a place of courage, even in the face of very real threats.
Naomi Klein

The ability to learn is the most important quality a leader can have.
Padmasree Warrior

Leadership is not a person or a position. It is a complex moral relationship between people based on trust, obligation, commitment, emotion, and a shared vision of the good.
Joanne Ciulla

One of the criticisms I've faced over the years is that I'm not aggressive enough or assertive enough or maybe somehow, because I'm empathetic, it means I'm weak. I totally rebel against that. I refuse to believe that you cannot be both compassionate and strong.
Jacinda Ardern

You are never too small to make a difference.
Greta Thunberg

If you're not making some notable mistakes along the way, you're certainly not taking enough business and career chances.
Sallie Krawcheck

We need to accept that we don't always make the right decisions, that we'll screw up royally sometimes. Understand that failure is not the opposite of success, it's part of success.
Arianna Huffington

Rarely are opportunities presented to you in a perfect way. In a nice little box with a yellow bow on top. "Here, open it, it's perfect. You'll love it." Opportunities — the good ones — are messy, confusing and hard to recognize. They're risky. They challenge you.
Susan Wojcicki

With kids, they don't do what you want them to do when you want them to do it. Organizations don't necessarily, either. You've got to listen. You've got to learn how to influence.
Ellen J. Kullman

There is no perfect fit when you're looking for the next big thing to do. You have to take opportunities and make an opportunity fit for you, rather than the other way around. The ability to learn is the most important quality a leader can have.
Sheryl Sandberg

It's okay to admit what you don't know. It's okay to ask for help. And it's more than okay to listen to the people you lead — in fact, it's essential.
Mary Barra

Magic happens when you connect people. I credit much of my success to always making it a point to truly get to know people and help them whenever I can. It's become the backbone of our firm's success. Women founders in particular are often highly skilled at making connections that can help advance their businesses.
Susan McPherson

I always did something I was a little not ready to do. I think that's how you grow. When there's that moment of "Wow, I'm not really sure I can do this," and you push through those moments, that's when you have a breakthrough.
Marissa Mayer

Who you are surrounded by often determines who you become.
Vicky Saunders

Leadership is hard to define, and good leadership even harder. But if you can get people to follow you to the ends of the earth, you are a great leader.
Indra Nooyi

Part of leadership is knowing when to go ahead with a decision that's within your authority because you're really convinced it's the right thing, even if other people don't understand it at that point.
Dr. Ingrid Mattson

Ninety percent of leadership is the ability to communicate something people want.
Dianne Feinstein

Emotional intelligence is the ability to use emotion to increase your own and others' success.
Annie McKee

People respond well to those that are sure of what they want.
Anna Wintour

Don't be intimidated by what you don't know. That can be your greatest strength and ensure that you do things differently from everyone else.
Sara Blakely

If you are committed to creating value and if you aren't afraid of hard times; obstacles become utterly unimportant. A nuisance perhaps; but with no real power. The world respects creation; people will get out of your way.
Candice Carpenter Olson

Leadership is about the team — the culture they keep and embrace, it's about empathy for your customers, clients, employees and the communities where you do business, it's about doing the right thing for the right reasons, being confident enough to take risks and responsible enough to think of those who your decisions and risks may affect.
Kat Cole

Do not be afraid to make decisions. Do not be afraid to make mistakes.
Carly Fiorina

Making the decision to not follow a system, or someone else's rules has allowed me to really dig into what my own strengths and gifts are without spending time feeling jaded or wasteful.
Ishita Gupta

A good leader is able to paint a picture of a vision for the future and then enlist others to go on the journey with her. A truly conscious leader recognizes that it is not about her, but that the team is looking to her for inspiration and direction. Keeping her ego in check is essential.
Tamra Ryan

You can and should set your own limits and clearly articulate them. This takes courage, but it is also liberating and empowering, and often earns you new respect.
Rosalind Brewer

I think it's a combination of personality traits that have helped me to succeed. Not only hard work — but patience, sacrifice and choosing my battles have all helped me to reach the point in my career to which I aspired, in a company I admired.
Katelyn Gleason

I have broken many glass ceilings — so I know it can be done.
Helen Clark

Cultivate a network of trusted mentors and colleagues. Other people can give us the best insight into ourselves — and our own limitations. We must have the courage to ask for help and to request feedback to expand our vision of what's possible.
Maria Castañón Moats

Continuous learning leads to continuous improvement. Commit yourself to advancing your knowledge, skills, and expertise. The business environment is quickly changing, and your understanding of the leading practices, thinking, and emerging tools will help you manage for better results. Be a lifelong student.
Pamela Gill Alabaster

I've always subscribed to the belief that the best leader is not one who has the most followers, but one who creates the most leaders. I strive every day — and in every program and offering we have at Integrous Women — to create more conscious, confident, and soulful leaders who, in return, will build a better world for all.
Stephanie Courtillier

I believe in a quiet, strong and grounded leadership. I think some of the best leaders are those whose work is widely known and respected but who, themselves, are relatively unknown.
Rachael Chong

Without passion, a person will have very little influence as a leader.
Michele Payn-Knoper

One bad day from one member of my staff doesn't mean they are not really good at their jobs the rest of the time. I play a long game in terms of management.
Helen McCabe

I don't go by the rule book. I lead from the heart, not the head.
Princess Diana

Never doubt that a small group of thoughtful committed citizens can change the world. Indeed, it is the only thing that ever has.
Margaret Mead

Women lead in different ways. Women rarely feel the need to speak the most at a meeting to make their point.
Patricia Bellinger

True leadership stems from individuality that is honestly and sometimes imperfectly expressed. Leaders should strive for authenticity over perfection.
Sheryl Sandberg

Just because you are CEO, don't think you have landed. You must continually increase your learning, the way you think, and the way you approach the organization.
Indra Nooyi

One of the most important things for any leader is to never let anyone else define who you are. And you define who you are. I never think of myself as being a woman CEO of this company. I think of myself as a steward of a great institution.
Ginni Rometty

I am nice. There's not such a thing as "too nice." But my expectations are high, and people do rise to my expectations. I don't manage based on fear. I manage based on expectations.
Marjorie Kaplan

Women are leaders everywhere you go, from the CEO who runs a Fortune 500 company to the housewife who raises her children and heads her household. Our country was built by strong women and we will continue to break down walls and defy stereotypes.
Nancy Pelosi

Strategic leaders must not get consumed by the operational and tactical side of their work. They have a duty to find time to shape the future.
Stephanie S. Mead

I know of no single formula for success. But over the years I have observed that some attributes of leadership are universal and are often about finding ways of encouraging people to combine their efforts, their talents, their insights, their enthusiasm and their inspiration to work together.
Queen Elizabeth II

I think leadership is service and there is power in that giving: to help people, to inspire and motivate them to reach their fullest potential.
Denise Morrison

Some leaders are born women.
Geraldine Ferraro

Leadership is a series of behaviors rather than a role for heroes.
Margaret Wheatley

Well-behaved women rarely make history.
Laurel Thatcher Ulrich

I'm tough, I'm ambitious, and I know exactly what I want. If that makes me a bitch, okay.
Madonna

True leaders understand that leadership is not about them but about those they serve. It is not about exalting themselves but about lifting others up.
Sheri L. Dew

Leadership should be born out of the understanding of the needs of those who would be affected by it.
Marian Anderson

Women have been trained to speak softly and carry a lipstick. Those days are over.
Bella Abzug

As a leader, it's a major responsibility on your shoulders to practice the behavior you want others to follow.
Himanshu Bhatia

Leadership is a two-way street, loyalty up and loyalty down. Respect for one's superiors; care for one's crew.
Admiral Grace Murray Hopper

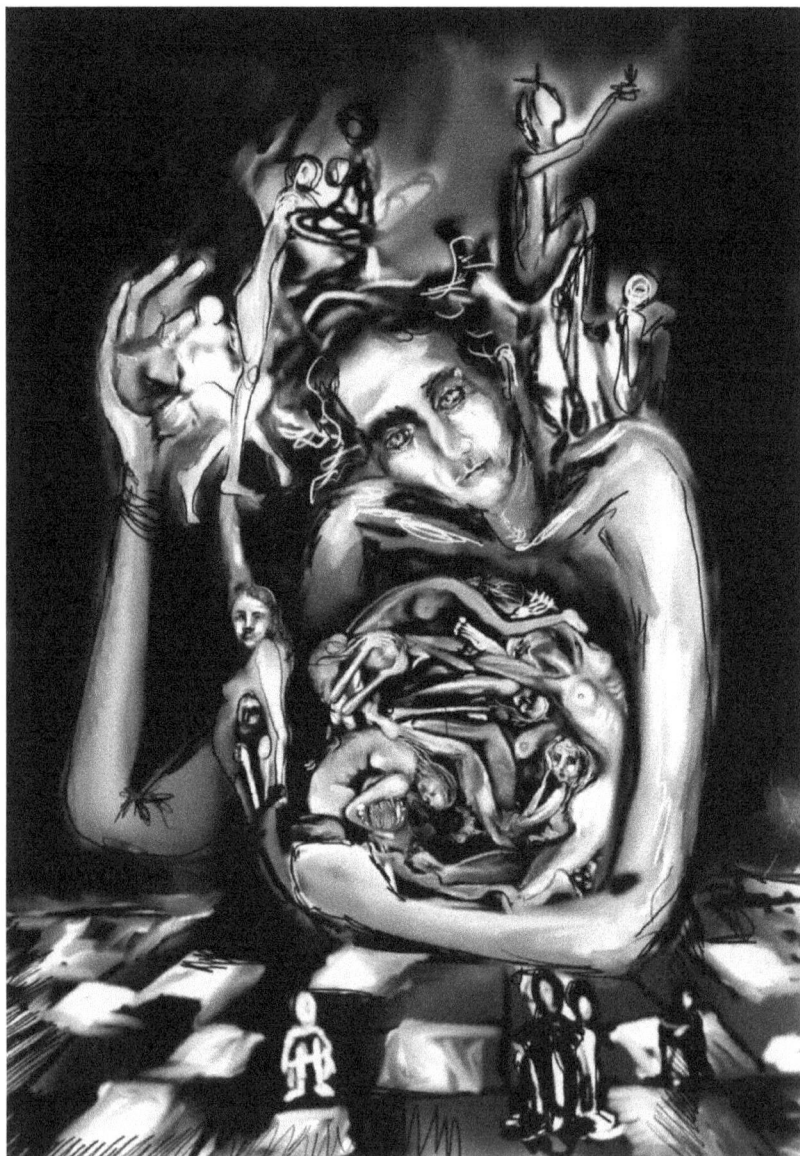

CHAPTER 2

Leading People

Adriana

The art of leading people is when you work with a team of people, positively influencing them with encouraging attitudes and behaviors, and always motivating them to work for a common goal.

Having the opportunity to lead people allows the professional growth of the group, the realization of new ventures, and the search for new opportunities for the good of all.

Leading people also requires strong communication skills. It is not only about defending new ideas and clearly explaining projects, but also knowing how to listen to others, something that many leaders do not know or put into practice. Finally, conflict resolution is important, as all leaders must have the ability for finding solutions to complex situations.

Steven

Great leaders know that sustainable, repeatable, replicable success results from collaborative, collective, and engaged efforts. This is why great leaders concentrate on the people side of success, including motivation, team building, group recognition, and group rewards.

People development is your number one priority as a leader. Developing your people is the single most important long-term priority and responsibility of all leaders at all levels of organizations.

To lead people effectively, leaders must take time to clearly communicate with their teams and team members. Doing so requires excellent and varied communications skills, for communicating is at the heart of leadership Almost by definition great leaders are great communicators. I cannot think of any great leaders who were poor communicators.

To handle yourself, use your head;
to handle others, use your heart.

Eleanor Roosevelt

Leading People Quotes

Kind words are short and easy to speak, but their echoes are truly endless.
Mother Teresa

He who angers you conquers you.
Elizabeth Kenny

There are two ways of spreading light: to be the candle or the mirror that reflects it.
Edith Wharton

Compromise: The art of dividing a cake in such a way that everybody believes they got the biggest piece.
Sherry Rothfield

Never ruin an apology with an excuse.
Kimberly Johnson

To handle yourself, use your head; to handle others, use your heart.
Eleanor Roosevelt

Pretend that every single person you meet has a sign around his or her neck that says, "Make me feel important." Not only will you succeed in sales, you will succeed in life.
Mary Kay Ash

The naked truth is always better than the best dressed lie.
Ann Landers

Saying nothing sometimes says the most.
Emily Dickinson

Our words should be purrs instead of hisses.
Kathrine Palmer Peterson

We should all know that diversity makes for a rich tapestry, and we must understand that all the threads of the tapestry are equal in value no matter what their color.
Maya Angelou

The practice of forgiveness is our most important contribution to the healing of the world.
Marianne Williamson

You should never let your fears prevent you from doing what you know is right.
Aung San Suu Kyi

Love and kindness are never wasted. They always make a difference. They bless the one who receives them, and they bless you, the giver.
Barbara De Angelis

You have to be first, different, or great.
Loretta Lynn

I think it's more fulfilling to be working with people.
Jean Stapleton

The ones that give, get back in kind.
Pam Durban

Do what you can to show you care about other people, and you will make our world a better place.
Rosalynn Carter

People do not wish to appear foolish. To avoid the appearance of foolishness, they are willing to remain actual fools.
Alice Walker

I praise loudly; I blame softly.
Catherine the Great

It seemed rather incongruous that in a society of super-sophisticated communication, we often suffer from a shortage of listeners.
Erma Bombeck

Forgiveness is the economy of the heart. Forgiveness saves the expense of anger, the cost of hatred, the waste of spirits.
Hannah More

Some of the shells that wash up on the beach were once very beautiful. You don't know what kind of journey they had to take to get them in their fragile shape. Same with people, be kind.
Linda Gifford

Small gestures can have a big impact. If you walk down the street and smile at someone, that will get passed on to the next person. That has the power to change someone's day.
Julianna Margulies

The true secret of giving advice is, after you have honestly given it, to be perfectly indifferent whether it is taken or not, and never persist in trying to set people right.
Hannah Whitall Smith

Instead of always harping on a man's faults, tell him of his virtues. Try to pull him out of his rut of bad habits. Hold up to him his better self, his real self that can dare and do and win out.
Eleanor H. Porter

The basic difference between being assertive and being aggressive is how our words and behavior affect the rights and wellbeing of others.
Sharon Anthony Bower

People are like stained-glass windows. They sparkle and shine when the sun is out, but when the darkness sets in their true beauty is revealed only if there is light from within.
Elisabeth Kübler-Ross

The people with whom you work reflect your own attitude. If you are suspicious, unfriendly and condescending, you will find these unlovely traits echoed all about you. But if you are on your best behavior, you will bring out the best in the persons with whom you are going to spend most of your waking hours.
Beatrice Vincent

When it comes to human dignity, we cannot make compromises.
Angela Merkel

Don't listen to people —— feel them. Lips may lie, hearts tell the truth.
Anita Krizzan

Whatever debases the intelligence degrades the entire human being.
Simone Weil

Every day use your magic to be of service to others.
Marcia Wieder

I've learned that people will forget what you said, people will forget what you did, but people will never forget how you made them feel.
Maya Angelou

Everyone has an invisible sign hanging from their neck saying "Make me feel important." Never forget this message when working with people.
Mary Kay Ash

The way your employees feel is the way your customers will feel. And if your employees don't feel valued, neither will your customers.
Sybil F. Stershic

We can improve our relationships with others by leaps and bounds if we become encouragers instead of critics.
Joyce Meyer

We are afraid to care too much, for fear that the other person does not care at all.
Eleanor Roosevelt

No matter how difficult and painful it may be, nothing sounds as good to the soul as truth.
Martha Beck

Fear is a natural reaction to moving closer to the truth.
Pema Chödrön

Before I can effectively discipline students, I have to earn their friendship and respect.
Marva Collins

Make no judgments where you have no compassion.
Anne McCaffrey

A pint can't hold a quart — if it holds a pint it is doing all that can be expected of it.
Margaret Deland

With any trial and circumstance, a person's true color either shines or darkens.
Shannon Walker

You cannot be fair to others without first being fair to yourself.
Vera Nazarian

If you want to see the true measure of a man, watch how he treats his inferiors, not his equals.
J. K. Rowling

There are two things people want more than sex and money... recognition and praise.
Mary Kay Ash

When virtues are pointed out first, flaws seem less insurmountable.
Judith Martin

Every human being is entitled to courtesy and consideration. Constructive criticism is not only to be expected but sought.
Margaret Chase Smith

When you surround yourself with smart people, they challenge you to think harder and in entirely different ways.
Marissa Mayer

Don't you dare underestimate the power of your own instinct.
Barbara Corcoran

Job training empowers people to realize their dreams and improve their lives.
Sylvia Matthews Burwell

When people go to work, they shouldn't have to leave their hearts at home.
Betty Bender

Culture is about performance, and making people feel good about how they contribute to the whole.
Tracy Streckenbach

Everyone wants to be appreciated, so if you appreciate someone, don't keep it a secret.
Mary Kay Ash

Employees who believe that management is concerned about them as a whole person — not just an employee — are more productive, more satisfied, more fulfilled. Satisfied employees mean satisfied customers, which leads to profitability.
Anne M. Mulcahy

Employees engage with employers and brand when they're treated as humans worthy of respect.
Meghan Biro

On what high-performing companies should be striving to create: A great place for great people to do great work.
Marilyn Carlson Nelson

People want to know they matter and they want to be treated as people. That's the new talent contract.
Pamela Stroko

Those who trust us educate us.
Mary Ann Evans

Nothing strengthens the judgment and quickens the conscience like individual responsibility.
Elizabeth Cady Stanton

Conflict leads to less-than-adequate performance, resentments, and lack of motivation.
Fran Rees

You're in a much better position to talk with people when they approach you than when you approach them.
Peace Pilgrim

Never underestimate the power of passion.
Eve Sawyer

Listening, not imitation, may be the sincerest form of flattery.
Dr. Joyce Brothers

A good listener is not someone with nothing to say. A good listener is a good talker with a sore throat.
Katharine Whitehorn

Saying nothing...sometimes says the most.
Emily Dickinson

You never really understand a person until you consider things from his point of view.
Harper Lee

It seemed rather incongruous that in a society of super sophisticated communication, we often suffer from a shortage of listeners.
Erma Bombeck

The trouble with talking too fast is you may say something you haven't thought of yet.
Ann Landers

Be careful because brazen behavior and a powerful mind can hide a delicate heart.
Imania Margria

No one can persuade another to change. Each of us guards a gate of change that can only be opened from the inside. We cannot open the gate of another, either by argument or emotional appeal.
Marilyn Ferguson

Appreciate the good things in a person, help him to nurture more. Ignore the bad qualities in a person, he will figure a way out from it only if we help him a little.
Bella Meraki

Good advice is always certain to be ignored, but that's no reason not to give it.
Agatha Christie

If human beings are perceived as potentials rather than problems, as possessing strengths instead of weaknesses, as unlimited rather that dull and unresponsive, then they thrive and grow to their capabilities.
Barbara Bush

I believe the greatest gift I can conceive of having from anyone is to be seen, heard, understood, and touched by them. The greatest gift I can give is to see, hear, understand, and touch another person.
Virginia Satir

When we fail to set boundaries and hold people accountable, we feel used and mistreated. This is why we sometimes attack who they are, which is far more hurtful than addressing a behavior or a choice.
Brené Brown

Making people feel important is precisely what a leader is paid for — because making people feel important motivates them to do better work.
Mary Kay Ash

Having powerful empathetic conversations is a critical piece of being a great manager.
Bianca McCann

You cannot define a person on just one thing. You can't just forget all these wonderful and good things that a person has done because one thing didn't come off the way you thought it should come off.
Aretha Franklin

Listening is a magnetic and strange thing, a creative force. You can see that when you think how the friends that really listen to us are the ones we move toward, and we want to sit in their radius as though it did us good.
Brenda Ueland

Motivation comes from working on things we care about. It also comes from working with people we care about.
Sheryl Sandberg

What I have learned is that people become motivated when you guide them to the source of their own power and when you make heroes out of employees who personify what you want to see in the organization.
Anita Roddick

If you don't give people a chance to fail, you won't innovate. If you want to be an innovative company, allow people to make mistakes.
Indra Nooyi

Everyone talks about building a relationship with your customer. I think you build one with your employees first.
Angela Ahrendts

The speed of the team is the speed of the boss.
Barbara Corcoran

It is only through conversation that we begin to understand differences and find common ground.
Molly Page

Put your ego in your pocket and sit on it.
Beverly Jenkins

We never know which lives we influence, or when, or why.
Laurie Buchanan

I define connection as the energy that exists between people when they feel seen, heard, and valued; when they can give and receive without judgment; and when they derive sustenance and strength from the relationship.
Brené Brown

The nice thing about teamwork is that you always have others on your side.
Margaret Carty

The smallest act in the most limited circumstances bears the seed of the same boundlessness, because one deed, and sometimes one word, suffices to change every constellation.
Hannah Arendt

Give credit where credit is due: simply said, if you want loyalty and best effort, you must be thoughtful.
Estée Lauder

A mentor is someone who allows you to see the hope inside yourself.
Oprah Winfrey

Ultimately, we can never change someone else's behavior — we can only change our own.
Jennifer Lopez

There is no such thing as self-respect without respect for others.
Pat Summitt

If you have knowledge, let others light their candles in it.
Margaret Fuller

Cooperation is the thorough conviction that nobody can get there unless everybody gets there.
Virginia Burden

Your legacy is every life you have ever touched.
Maya Angelou

You take people as far as they will go, not as far as you would like them to go.
Jeannette Rankin

You cannot hope to build a better world without improving the individuals. To that end, each of us must work for his own improvement, and at the same time share a general responsibility for all humanity, our particular duty being to aid those to whom we think we can be most useful.
Marie Curie

I do not think that the banks of a river suffer because they let the river flow.
Frida Kahlo

In the absence of feedback, people will fill in the blanks with a negative. They will assume you don't like them.
Pat Summitt

I wish that more women realized that helping another woman win, cheering her on, praying for her, or sharing a resource with her does not take away from the blessings coming to them. In fact, the more you give, the more you receive. Empowering women doesn't come from selfishness, but rather from selflessness.
Selene Kinder

CHAPTER 3

Self-Development

Adriana

Self-development refers to the commitment of a person to think and decide for themselves. This implies the discovery of new skills and the repetition of actions to improve habits and personal skills every day.

An individual who is committed to self-development must have a clear vision about their goal and must be attentive to all the opportunities that come their way. You need to have a strategic life plan and act creatively and innovatively to achieve all of your goals.

Self-development can be achieved with work, self-criticism, studies, and updating of knowledge. It also requires an important sense of personal responsibility and a proactive and positive attitude all the time.

To achieve self-development, self-knowledge is key. This includes knowing and recognizing oneself and committing to a reflective process through which a person acquires an understanding of their own strengths and areas for improvement. This allows them to take advantage of opportunities and be prepared for the challenges presented in life.

Steven

Your personal development is you own responsibility — not that of the organization you work for, your boss, the HR department, or anyone else.

It is time to stop waiting for your company to develop your skills. Likewise, do not waste time on programs full of theory but no practicality.

Be proactive. Start leading and controlling your own personal and professional development.

Additionally, you should never wait for anyone to tell you how to develop yourself. You already have an intrinsic inkling as to your development areas. And don't focus only on what you see as gap areas. Continue to build your strengths and use these to leverage your performance and improvement

And remember, never stop learning, for life never stops teaching.

Learn to get in touch with the silence within yourself and know that everything in this life has a purpose.
There are no mistakes, no coincidences.
All events are given to us to learn from.

Elisabeth Kübler-Ross

Self-Development Quotes

And the day came when the risk to remain tight in a bud was more painful than the risk it took to blossom.
Anaïs Nin

When one door of happiness closes, another opens, but often we look so long at the closed door that we do not see the one that has been opened for us.
Helen Keller

Nobody can go back and start a new beginning, but anyone can start today and make a new ending.
Maria Robinson

A year from now you may wish you had started today.
Karen Lamb

People throw away what they could have by insisting on perfection, which they cannot have, and looking for it where they will never find it.
Edith Schaeffer

It isn't until you come to a spiritual understanding of who you are — not necessarily a religious feeling, but deep down, the spirit within — that you can begin to take control.
Oprah Winfrey

Without dreams we couldn't live.
Kara Melancon

A life of reaction is a life of slavery, intellectually and spiritually. One must strive for a life of action, not reaction.
Rita Mae Brown

Learn to get in touch with the silence within yourself and know that everything in this life has a purpose. There are no mistakes, no coincidences. All events are given to us to learn from.
Elisabeth Kübler-Ross

Beyond anything else, listen to yourself. You are meant to discover reality from inside and to direct your life in this way. As you begin to live according to your own guidance and your own daring, everything changes completely.
Barbara Marciniak

Light tomorrow with today!
Elizabeth Barrett Browning

You do what you have to do, to do what you want to do.
Patricia Fripp

Don't limit yourself. Many people limit themselves to what they think they can do. You can go as far as you mind lets you. What you believe, you can achieve.
Mary Kay Ash

From your parents you learn love and laughter and how to put one foot before the other but when books are opened you discover you have wings.
Helen Hayes

Face your deficiencies and acknowledge them; but do not let them master you. Let them teach you patience, sweetness and insight.
Helen Keller

A creative man is motivated by the desire to achieve, not by the desire to beat others.
Ayn Rand

No person is your friend who demands your silence, or denies your right to grow.
Alice Walker

Unless you know what you want, you can't ask for it.
Emma Albani

As you become more clear about who you really are, you'll be better able to decide what is best for you the first time around.
Oprah Winfrey

When you know yourself you are empowered. When you accept yourself you are invincible.
Tina Lifford

If you're able to be yourself, then you have no competition.
Barbara Cook

You have to be first, different, or great.
Loretta Lynn

Sometime in your life you will go on a journey. It will be the longest journey you have ever taken. It is the journey to find yourself.
Katherine Sharp

Maturity includes the recognition that no one is going to see anything in us that we don't see in ourselves. Stop waiting for a producer. Produce yourself.
Marianne Williamson

What we really want to do is what we are really meant to do. When we do what we are meant to do, money comes to us, doors open for us, we feel useful, and the work we do feels like play to us.
Julia Cameron

If we don't change, we don't grow. If we don't grow, we aren't really living.
Gail Sheehy

There is no paycheck that can equal the feeling of contentment that comes from being the person you are meant to be.
Oprah Winfrey

That's the risk you take if you change: that people you've been involved with won't like the new you. But other people who do will come along.
Lisa Alther

There is no agony like bearing an untold story inside of you.
Maya Angelou

What the world needs now is for each of us to be who we truly are, and to bring our gifts into the world. Don't hold back any longer. Be Present. Be You. That is enough. Really it is.
Nancy Bishop

You are unique, and if that is not fulfilled, then something has been lost.
Martha Graham

Always be a first-rate version of yourself, instead of a second-rate version of somebody else.
Judy Garland

Love yourself first and everything else falls into line. You really have to love yourself to get anything done in this world.
Lucille Ball

You have been criticizing yourself for years, and it hasn't worked. Try approving of yourself and see what happens.
Louise L. Hay

Invest in yourself, in your education. There's nothing better.
Sylvia Porter

One of the things about equality is not just that you be treated equally to a man, but that you treat yourself equally to the way you treat a man.
Marlo Thomas

It is never too late to be what you might have been.
Mary Ann Evans

As our knowledge is converted to wisdom, the door to opportunity is unlocked.
Barbara Winder

Take responsibility for yourself...because no one's going to take responsibility for you.
Tyra Banks

Just remember, you can do anything you set your mind to, but it takes action, perseverance and facing your fears.
Gillian Anderson

I was always looking outside myself for strength and confidence but it comes from within. It is there all the time.
Anna Freud

Character is what emerges from all the little things you were too busy to do yesterday, but did anyway.
Mignon McLaughlin

Adversity precedes growth.
Rosemarie Rossetti

Until you make peace with who you are, you will never be content with what you have.
Doris Mortman

If you do not tell the truth about yourself you cannot tell it about other people.
Virginia Woolf

Nothing ever goes away until it has taught us what we need to know.
Pema Chödrön

I wasn't afraid to fail. Something good always comes out of failure.
Anne Baxter

Practice is the hardest part of learning, and training is the essence of transformation.
Ann Voskamp

The truth you believe and cling to makes you unavailable to hear anything new.
Pema Chödrön

Change is inevitable. Growth is intentional.
Glenda Cloud

We are not what we know but what we are willing to learn.
Mary Catherine Bateson

You are the product of your own brainstorm.
Rosemary Konner Steinbaum

The excitement of learning separates youth from old age. As long as you're learning, you're not old.
Rosalyn S. Yalow

Lineage, personality, and environment may shape you, but they do not define your full potential.
Mollie Marti

The thing that makes you say, "I want to do something" — that is the beginning of talent.
Stella Adler

Growth is a spiral process, doubling back on itself, reassessing and regrouping.
Julia Cameron

Some people thrive on huge, dramatic change. Some people prefer the slow and steady route. Do what's right for you.
Julie Morgenstern

Don't ever wait around for someone else to tell you how to develop yourself.
April Arnzen

Talk to yourself like you would to someone you love.
Brené Brown

If you were born without wings, do nothing to prevent them from growing.
Coco Chanel

Embrace what you don't know, especially in the beginning, because what you don't know can become your greatest asset. It ensures that you will absolutely be doing things different from everybody else.
Sara Blakely

No matter who you are, no matter what you did, no matter where you've come from, you can always change, become a better version of yourself.
Madonna

Sometimes you don't realize your own strength until you come face to face with your greatest weakness.
Susan Gale

Do one thing every day that scares you.
Eleanor Roosevelt

One must learn to be silent just as one must learn to talk.
Virginia Woolf

The way you treat yourself sets the standard for others.
Sonya Friedman

Learn. Know what you didn't know before.
Eileen Fisher

We do not need magic to change the world. We carry all the power we need inside ourselves already: We have the power to imagine better.
J. K. Rowling

Where there is no struggle, there is no strength.
Oprah Winfrey

Vulnerability is the birthplace of innovation, creativity, and change.
Brené Brown

Every small positive change we make in ourselves repays us in confidence in the future.
Alice Walker

Sometimes you have to be alone to truly know your worth.
Karen A. Baquiran

Belief in oneself is incredibly infectious. It generates momentum, the collective force of which far outweighs any kernel of self-doubt that may creep in.
Aimee Mullins

It takes A LOT of energy — mentally and sometimes physically — to move in a new direction.
Karen Watts

No one is in control of your happiness but you; therefore, you have the power to change anything about yourself or your life that you want to change.
Barbara De Angelis

If you are facing a new challenge or being asked to do something that you have never done before don't be afraid to step out. You have more capability than you think you do but you will never see it unless you place a demand on yourself for more.
Joyce Meyer

A life filled with vicissitudes, uncertainty and hard lessons provides us with skills to better approach new challenges that come along.
Vivian Eisenecher

Challenges are an opportunity to test you and rise to the next level.
Angelica Montrose

Only make decisions that support your self-image, self-esteem, and self-worth.
Oprah Winfrey

Life's challenges are not supposed to paralyze you, they're supposed to help you discover who you are.
Bernice Johnson Reagon

When we give ourselves permission to fail, we, at the same time, give ourselves permission to excel.
Eloise Ristad

To uncover your true potential, you must first find your own limits and then you have to have the courage to blow past them.
Picabo Street

Become your best self by investing in your education, finding positive aspects in adverse situations, and fulfilling your life purpose.
Irina Zlatogorova

Dream and give yourself permission to envision a you that you choose to be.
Joy Page

It's never too late – never too late to start over, never too late to be happy.
Jane Fonda

You can't turn back the clock. But you can wind it up again.
Bonnie Prudden

All change is not growth, as all movement is not forward.
Ellen Glasgow

You can never meet your potential until you truly learn to love yourself.
Teresa Collins

Take your life into your own hands, and what happens? A terrible thing, no one to blame.
Erica Jong

I give myself, sometimes, admirable advice, but I am incapable of taking it.
Mary Wortley Montagu

The inner fire is the most important thing mankind possesses.
Edith Södergran

Motivation is a battle for the heart, not just an appeal to the mind. Passion is always an expression of the soul.
Patricia Dixon

All knowledge is worth having.
Jacqueline Carey

You're better than this. Better than whatever it is you're going to do now.
Richelle Mead

Self-esteem is earned! When you dare to dream, dare to follow that dream, dare to suffer through the pain, sacrifice, self-doubts, and friction from the world — when you show such courage and tenacity — you will genuinely impress yourself. And most important, you will treat yourself accordingly and not settle for less from others — at least, not for long.
Laura Schlessinger

The strongest principle of growth lies in the human choice.
Mary Ann Evans

Growth is an erratic forward movement: two steps forward, one step back. Remember that and be very gentle with yourself.
Julia Cameron

What is your purpose, what is your calling? What I know for sure is, if you ask the question the answer will come. You have to be willing to listen for the answer. You have to get still enough to hear it and pay attention, to be fully conscious enough to see not just with your eyes but through them to the truth of who you are and what you can be.
Oprah Winfrey

The willingness to accept responsibility for one's own life is the source from which self-respect springs.
Joan Didion

The only questions that really matter are the ones you ask yourself.
Ursula Kroeber Le Guin

The self is made, not given.
Barbara Myerhoff

You have to be absolutely frank with yourself. Face your handicaps; don't try to hide them. Instead, develop something else.
Audrey Hepburn

Embrace what you don't know, especially in the beginning, because what you don't know can become your greatest asset. It ensures that you will absolutely be doing things different from everybody else.
Sara Blakely

Choose to focus your time, energy, and conversation around people who inspire you, support you, and help you to grow you into your happiest, strongest, wisest self.
Karen Salmansohn

You realize yourself when you start reflecting.
Lauren Bacall

I restore myself when I'm alone. A career is born in public — talent in privacy.
Marilyn Monroe

Strive for authenticity over perfection.
Sheryl Sandberg

Stop wearing your wishbone where your backbone ought to be.
Elizabeth Gilbert

Don't compromise yourself. You are all you've got.
Janis Joplin

It's one thing for other people to see potential in you, and it's quite another for you to understand that and see it in yourself.
Daisy Ridley

There are multiple sides to all of us. Who we are — and who we might be if we follow our dreams.
Miley Cyrus

When your clarity meets your conviction and you apply action to the equation, your world will begin to transform before your eyes.
Lisa Nichols

Becoming is better than being.
Carol Dweck

I learned to always take on things I'd never done before. Growth and comfort do not coexist.
Ginni Rometty

Sometimes you find out what you are supposed to be doing by doing the things you are not supposed to do.
Oprah Winfrey

Self-transformation is not five minutes from now; it's a present activity. In this moment you can make a different choice, and it's these small choices and successes that build up over time to help cultivate a healthy self-image and self-esteem.
Jillian Michaels

Low self-confidence isn't a life sentence. Self-confidence can be learned, practiced, and mastered — just like any other skill. Once you master it, everything in your life will change for the better.
Barrie Davenport

You have to know what sparks the light in you so that you, in your own way, can illuminate the world.
Oprah Winfrey

Having compassion starts and ends with having compassion for all those unwanted parts of ourselves.
Pema Chödrön

Never be limited by other people's limited imaginations.
Mae Jemison

Many receive advice, only the wise profit from it.
Harper Lee

If you only think about your own advancement, your own success, you run out of fuel pretty quickly. But if we believed in something bigger than ourselves, that kind of motivation is self-sustaining.
Elaine Chao

As one goes through life, one learns that if you don't paddle your own canoe, you don't move.
Katharine Hepburn

CHAPTER 4

Mindset

Adriana

Each person has a collection of personal ideas and convictions that comprise their overall vision of life. Such ideas and convictions are the foundation of a mindset.

It could be said that the mentality of each individual is their way of understanding the very existence of this world.

Also, when we talk about mental state, it is really a challenge, because we know that the mind dominates the body. Everything we think we attract and, sooner or later, our thoughts are manifested in our life.

For this reason, it is very important to exercise the mind daily with positive thoughts, pleasant reading, meditation, and many other things that will enable our mental state find a balance. The results of this will be reflected in our day-to-day activities, behaviors, actions, and thoughts.

In the same way, the people we allow to be close to us will always negatively or positively influence our mood. So, we must be very careful in choosing the people around us and always seek happiness as the best state for our mind, body, and soul.

Steven

Know thyself.

Those words inscribed in gold letters on the Temple of Apollo at Delphi, are the most important two-word phrase ever written.

A mindset of self-understanding means grasping how your feelings, emotions, and thoughts are impacting your actions, behaviors, and decisions. It means having a definite grasp of your strengths and weaknesses, as well as an elevated sense of what motivates, de-motivates, satisfies, delights, annoys, and angers you.

Your mindset reflects your beliefs, attitudes, and expectations. Based on your beliefs and principles, your mindset determines how you view situations, people, and events. It governs where you place your focus.

A fixed mindset believes talent and abilities are innate, permanent, and resistant to effort. A growth mindset understands that effort, learning from failure, and perseverance can improve performance. Have a growth mindset!

The thoughts we choose to think
are the tools we use to paint the canvas of our lives.

Louise L. Hay

Mindset Quotes

Each day offers us the gift of being a special occasion if we can simply learn that, as well as giving, it is wise to receive with grace and a grateful heart.
Sarah Ban Breathnach

I find that it is not the circumstances in which we are placed, but the spirit in which we face them, that constitutes our comfort.
Elizabeth T. King

The purpose of our lives is to give birth to the best which is within us.
Marianne Williamson

No matter what age you are, or what your circumstances might be, you are special, and you still have something unique to offer. Your life, because of who you are, has meaning.
Barbara De Angelis

Make it a rule of life never to regret. Regret is an appalling waste of energy — you can't build on it; it's only for wallowing in.
Katherine Mansfield

Belief in oneself is one of the most important bricks in building any successful venture.
Lydia M. Child

We can have it all, but not at the same time.
Patricia Fripp

I think the key is for women not to set any limits.
Martina Navratilova

You gain strength, courage and confidence by every experience in which you really stop to look fear in the face. You are able to say to yourself, "I lived through this horror. I can take the next thing that comes along." You must do the thing you think you cannot do.
Eleanor Roosevelt

When we do the best that we can, we never know what miracle is wrought in our life, or in the life of another.
Helen Keller

The sign of intelligent people is their ability to control emotions by the application of reason.
Marya Mannes

I'm not happy, I'm cheerful. There's a difference. A happy woman has no cares at all. A cheerful woman has cares but has learned how to deal with them.
Beverly Sills

My mission in life is not merely to survive, but to thrive; and to do so with some passion, some compassion, some humor, and some style.
Maya Angelou

If you resist change, you will face challenges on a daily basis. If you consciously refocus your attitude to see the benefits of change, your outlook becomes positive and life becomes easier.
Catherine Pulsifer

We can always choose to perceive things differently. You can focus on what's wrong in your life, or you can focus on what's right.
Marianne Williamson

Power is the ability to do good things for others.
Brooke Astor

You can't shake hands with a clenched fist.
Indira Gandhi

The thoughts we choose to think are the tools we use to paint the canvas of our lives.
Louise L. Hay

Look at everything as though you were seeing it either for the first or last time.
Betty Smith

No pessimist ever discovered the secret of the stars nor sailed to an uncharted land nor opened a new heaven to the human spirit.
Helen Keller

I always feel sorry for people who think more about a rainy day ahead than sunshine today.
Elinor Denniston

One of the things I learned the hard way was that it doesn't pay to get discouraged. Keeping busy and making optimism a way of life can restore your faith in yourself.
Lucille Ball

Reject hatred without hating.
Mary Baker Eddy

Achievement doesn't come from what we do, but from who we are.
Marianne Williamson

You're always with yourself, so you might as well enjoy the company.
Diane von Furstenberg

Never bend your head. Always hold it high. Look the world straight in the face.
Helen Keller

If you don't like something, change it. If you can't change it, change your attitude. Don't complain.
Maya Angelou

Age is not a handicap. Age is nothing but a number. It is how you use it.
Ethel Payne

Life is too precious to be spent in this weaving and unweaving of false impressions.
Mary Ann Evans

Remember that not to be happy is not to be grateful.
Elizabeth Carter

Never regret. If it's good, it's wonderful. If it's bad, it's experience.
Eleanor Hibbert

To err is human, but it feels divine.
Mae West

There is no chance, no destiny, no fate that can circumvent or hinder or control the firm resolve of a determined soul.
Ella Wheeler Wilcox

There are no hopeless situations, only people who are hopeless about them.
Dinah Shore

Our deepest fear is not that we are inadequate. Our deepest fear is that we are powerful beyond measure.
Marianne Williamson

There are years that ask questions and years that answer.
Zora Neale Hurston

Don't limit yourself. Many people limit themselves to what they think they can do.
Mary Kay Ash

We may encounter many defeats, but we must not be defeated.
Maya Angelou

There are no mistakes, only opportunities.
Tina Fey

You're imperfect, and you're wired for struggle, but you are worthy of love and belonging.
Brené Brown

Dwelling on the negative simply contributes to its power.
Shirley MacLaine

It isn't what happens to us that causes us to suffer; it's what we say to ourselves about what happens.
Pema Chödrön

If you don't like something, change it; if you can't change it, change the way you think about it.
Mary Engelbreit

Change is not only likely, it's inevitable.
Barbara Sher

I have learned over the years that when one's mind is made up, this diminishes fear.
Rosa Parks

You cannot have a positive life and a negative mind.
Joyce Meyer

And we have complete control over our own attitude. We are the ones we decide how we feel, how we look at things, how we react.
Catherine Pulsifer

I discovered I always have choices and sometimes it's only a choice of attitude.
Judith M. Knowlton

How we feel about ourselves is a choice, although it often doesn't feel that way.
Anna Lind Thomas

You are your possibilities. If you know that, you can do anything.
Oprah Winfrey

Don't compare yourself to someone else's highlight reel.
Kimberly O'Connor

A positive attitude from you tends to produce a positive attitude toward you.
Deborah Day

Realize that if a door closed, it's because what was behind it wasn't meant for you.
Mandy Hale

Hope is a renewable option: If you run out of it at the end of the day, you get to start over in the morning.
Barbara Kingsolver

Nothing in life is to be feared, it is only to be understood. Now is the time to understand more, so that we may fear less.
Marie Curie

Disappointment is really just a term for our refusal to look on the bright side.
Richelle E. Goodrich

I am strong. I am beautiful. I am enough.
Vanessa Pawlowski

To dream is to have your own world you created in you're in your mind but you have to unleash that world to the real world for everyone to benefit from it and also for your own benefit to grow and succeed.
Euginia Herlihy

Could we change our attitude, we should not only see life differently, but life itself would come to be different. Life would undergo a change of appearance because we ourselves had undergone a change of attitude.
Katherine Mansfield

Never believe that you are anything less than extraordinary.
Kaiden Blake

Self-approval and self-acceptance in the now are the main keys to positive changes in every area of our lives.
Louise L. Hay

My grandmother told me that every good thing I do helps some human being in the world. I believed her 50 years ago, and I still do.
Maya Angelou

I avoid looking forward or backward, and try to keep looking upward.
Charlotte Brontë

We cannot always control our thoughts, but we can control our words, and repetition impresses the subconscious, and we are then master of the situation.
Florence Scovel Shinn

How you react emotionally is a choice in any situation.
Judith Orloff

Speak positivity to yourself daily and repeatedly. You can manifest positivity into your life simply by speaking it and believing it.
Gabriella Marigold Lindsay

After all, tomorrow is another day.
Scarlett O'Hara

We must overcome the notion that we must be regular...it robs you of the chance to be extraordinary and leads you to the mediocre.
Uta Hagen

Hope costs nothing.
Colette

The greatest lesson of life is that you are responsible for your life.
Oprah Winfrey

Long ago, I made up my mind that when things were said involving only me, I would pay no attention to them, except when valid criticism was carried by which I could profit.
Eleanor Roosevelt

To be passive is to let others decide for you. To be aggressive is to decide for others. To be assertive is to decide for yourself. And to trust that there is enough, that you are enough.
Edith Eva Eger

Surrender to what is. Let go of what was. Have faith in what will be.
Sonia Ricotti

Humility is about refusing to get all tangled up with yourself. It's about surrender, receptivity, awareness, simplicity. Breathing in. Breathing out.
Cheryl Strayed

If you don't like something change it; if you can't change it, change the way you think about it.
Mary Engelbreit

What people in the world think of you is really none of your business.
Martha Graham

A positive attitude gives you power over your circumstances instead of your circumstances having power over you.
Joyce Meyer

You are the only person who thinks in your mind! You are the power and the authority in your world.
Louise L. Hay

Imagination belongs to hope. It's the creative dance of possibility.
Sharon Weil

You won't be happy, whatever you do, unless you're comfortable with your own conscience.
Lucille Ball

Decide whether or not the goal is worth the risks involved. If it is, stop worrying.
Amelia Earhart

If you can't make it better, you can laugh at it.
Erma Bombeck

Could we change our attitude, we should not only see life differently, but life itself would come to be different. Life would undergo a change of appearance because we ourselves had undergone a change of attitude.
Katherine Mansfield

Act the way you want to feel.
Gretchen Rubin

Gratitude turns what we have into enough, and more. It turns denial into acceptance, chaos into order, confusion into clarity. It makes sense of our past, brings peace for today, and creates a vision for tomorrow.
Melody Beattie

Be your own artist, and always be confident in what you're doing. If you're not going to be confident, you might as well not be doing it.
Aretha Franklin

Don't beat yourself up if you do something stupid. Let it go. Nothing is an important as it seems. Try to look at the big picture and get a different perspective.
Ellen DeGeneres

It's a new day. Count your blessings, think twice before you complain, give more than you ask for, do what makes you happy and enjoy life.
Ariana Grande

Doubt is a killer. You just have to know who you are and what you stand for.
Jennifer Lopez

I have learned over the years that when one's mind is made up, this diminishes fear.
Rosa Parks

Success is a state of mind. If you want success start thinking of yourself as a success.
Dr. Joyce Brothers

All sorrows can be borne if you tell a story about them.
Karen Blixen

Only when we are no longer afraid, do we begin to live.
Dorothy Thompson

You can often change your circumstances by changing your attitude.
Eleanor Roosevelt

Very early, I knew that the only object in life was to grow.
Margaret Fuller

Always remember that you are absolutely unique. Just like everybody else.
Margaret Mead

The beginning is always today.
Mary Wollstonecraft Shelley

We can make ourselves miserable or we can make ourselves strong. The amount of effort is the same.
Pema Chödrön

If there's anything you've wanted to do for yourself, just get out and go for it.
Arlene Pieper

Regardless of how you feel inside, always try to look like a winner. Even if you are behind, a sustained look of control and confidence can give you a mental edge that results in victory.
Diane Arbus

Resilience is accepting your new reality, even if it's less good than the one you had before. You can fight it, you can do nothing but scream about what you've lost, or you can accept that and try to put together something that's good.
Elizabeth Edwards

The excursion is the same when you go looking for your sorrow as when you go looking for your joy.
Eudora Welty

Beauty begins the moment you decide to be yourself.
Coco Chanel

If you accept a limiting belief, then it will become a truth for you.
Louise L. Hay

Generosity is the best investment.
Diane von Furstenberg

Keep your face in the sunshine and you can never see the shadow.
Helen Keller

The way you tell your story to yourself matters.
Amy Cuddy

Today was a good one. I hope tomorrow is a repeat performance.
Linda Poindexter

All battles are first won or lost in the mind.
Joan of Arc

The regrets of yesterday and the fear of tomorrow can kill you.
Liza Minnelli

To plant a garden is to believe in tomorrow.
Audrey Hepburn

Some days are just bad days, that's all. You have to experience sadness to know happiness, and I remind myself that not every day is going to be a good day, that's just the way it is!
Dita Von Teese

Fear is stupid. So are regrets.
Marilyn Monroe

The greatest discovery of all time is that a person can change his future by merely changing his attitude.
Oprah Winfrey

Being confident and believing in your own self-worth is necessary to achieving your potential.
Sheryl Sandberg

People think being alone makes you lonely, but I don't think that's true. Being surrounded by the wrong people is the loneliest thing in the world.
Kim Culbertson

Face your deficiencies and acknowledge them but do not let them master you.
Helen Keller

Fearlessness is like a muscle. I know from my own life that the more I exercise it, the more natural it becomes to not let my fears run me.
Arianna Huffington

The greatest mistake you can ever make in life is to be continually fearing you will make one.
Ellen Hubbard

The practice of forgiveness is our most important contribution to the healing of the world.
Marianne Williamson

Either they like you or they don't. Never try to convince somebody of your worth. If a person doesn't appreciate you, they don't deserve you. Respect yourself and be with people who truly value you.
Brigitte Nicole

Feeling grateful or appreciative of someone or something in your life actually attracts more of the things that you appreciate and value into your life.
Christiane Northrup

The most difficult times for many of us are the ones we give ourselves.
Pema Chödrön

Remember, no one can make you feel inferior without your consent.
Eleanor Roosevelt

What can I do today to shine my light even brighter?
Leonie Dawson

The question isn't who is going to let me; it's who is going to stop me.
Ayn Rand

Kindness is always fashionable.
Amelia Barr

What would you do if you weren't afraid?
Sheryl Sandberg

I am not afraid of storms, for I am learning how to sail my ship.
Louisa May Alcott

Optimism is the faith that leads to achievement. Nothing can be done without hope and confidence.
Helen Keller

Don't let compliments get to your head and don't let criticism get to your heart.
Lysa TerKeurst

Optimism is a happiness magnet. If you stay positive, good things and good people will be drawn to you.
Mary Lou Retton

The most important thing in your life is to live your life with integrity and to not give into peer pressure to try to be something that you're not.
Ellen DeGeneres

There is always time to make right what is wrong.
Susan Griffin

The purpose of life is to live it, to taste experience to the utmost, to reach out eagerly and without fear for newer and richer experience.
Eleanor Roosevelt

Life is not measured by the number of breaths we take, but by the moments that take our breath away.
Maya Angelou

In the end, people will judge you anyway, so don't live your life impressing others — live your life impressing yourself.
Eunice Camacho Infante

Stay committed to your visions and dreams.
Lailah Gifty Akita

Our deepest fear is not that we are inadequate. Our deepest fear is that we are powerful beyond measure. It is our light, not our darkness, that most frightens us. We ask ourselves, "Who am I to be brilliant, gorgeous, talented, fabulous?" Actually, who are you *not* to be? You are a child of God. Your playing small doesn't serve the world.
Marianne Williamson

CHAPTER 5

Success

Adriana

Like many individuals who are always in constant search of success, your thoughts about success will be the key to achieving it. As I mentioned in the previous category, our thoughts define our reality. For this reason, the ideal is always to think about success and the achievements that we can attain in the short, medium, and long term.

You should regularly reflect on your mission in life in order to be clear about your objectives and how to use your gifts. Regardless of your interests, passion, hobbies, or tastes, you must think that you will accomplish what you want to achieve.

Remember, life is short and we must not waste time with negative thoughts, which hinder our desires to achieve success.

Steven

Thanks to the self-help and personal development industries, there are probably more words written on success than any other subject. And, as you can imagine, there are as many definitions of success as there are authors.

For me, the best definition of success comes from legendary UCLA basketball coach John Wooden, "Success is peace of mind which is a direct result of self-satisfaction in knowing you did your best to become the best that you are capable of becoming."

I see success as an on-going process of becoming better. Of striving to become the best that you are truly capable of being in whatever endeavors you choose. Successful people are always expanding and improving themselves — intellectually, spiritually, emotionally, and physically.

We each have options about what we will do with our lives and what we will make of ourselves. However, no matter what paths we choose or what options we select, once those decisions are made, we have two choices: 1) to be less than what we have the capacity to become, or 2) to be all that we can be, to strive as best we can with the skills we have and the circumstances given.

Life is not easy for any of us. But what of that?
We must have perseverance and above all
confidence in ourselves.
We must believe that we are gifted for something
and that this thing must be attained.

Marie Curie

Success Quotes

The doors we open and close each day decide the lives we live.
Flora Whittemore

The purpose of our lives is to give birth to the best that is in us. It is only through our own personal awakening that the world can be awakened. We cannot give what we do not have.
Marianne Williamson

One act of beneficence, one act of real usefulness, is worth all the abstract sentiment in the world.
Ann Radcliffe

Give yourself something to work toward — constantly.
Mary Kay Ash

To aim at the best and to remain essentially ourselves is one and the same thing.
Janet Erskine Stuart

If you have a talent, use it in every way possible. Don't hoard it. Don't dole it out like a miser. Spend it lavishly, like a millionaire intent on going broke.
Brenda Francis

People seldom see the halting and painful steps by which the most insignificant success is achieved.
Anne Sullivan

Why not be oneself? That is the whole secret of a successful appearance. If one is a greyhound, why try to look like a Pekinese?
Edith Sitwell

I didn't have the same fitness or ability as the other girls, so I had to beat them with my mind.
Martina Hingis

Life is my college. May I graduate well, and earn some honors.
Louisa May Alcott

You can't just sit there and wait for people to give you that golden dream. You've got to get out there and make it happen for yourself.
Diana Ross

Creativity is inventing, experimenting, growing, taking risks, breaking rules, making mistakes and having fun.
Mary Lou Cook

Don't wait for your "ship to come in" and feel angry and cheated when it doesn't. Get going with something small.
Irene Kassorla

One can never consent to creep when one feels an impulse to soar.
Helen Keller

Life is to be lived. If you have to support yourself, you had bloody well better find some way that is going to be interesting. And you don't do that by sitting around.
Katharine Hepburn

Be more splendid, more extraordinary. Use every moment to fill yourself up.
Oprah Winfrey

You must learn a new way to think before you can master a new way to be.
Marianne Williamson

We delight in the beauty of the butterfly, but rarely admit the changes it has gone through to achieve that beauty.
Maya Angelou

We gain strength, and courage, and confidence by each experience in which we really stop to look fear in the face...we must do that which we think we cannot.
Eleanor Roosevelt

I always wondered why somebody didn't do something about that, then I realized I was somebody.
Lily Tomlin

Creative minds have always been known to survive any kind of bad training.
Anna Freud

Be of good cheer. Do not think of today's failures, but of the success that may come tomorrow. You have set yourselves a difficult task, but you will succeed if you persevere; and you will find a joy in overcoming obstacles.
Helen Keller

Life is not easy for any of us. But what of that? We must have perseverance and above all confidence in ourselves. We must believe that we are gifted for something and that this thing must be attained.
Marie Curie

If you have love in your life, it can make up for a great many things you lack. If you don't have it, no matter what else there is, it is not enough.
Ann Landers

If you're never scared or embarrassed or hurt, it means you never take any chances.
Julia Sorel

Nourish beginnings.
Murial Rukeyser

More important than talent, strength, or knowledge is the ability to laugh at yourself and enjoy the pursuit of your dreams.
Amy Grant

Follow your instincts. That's where true wisdom manifests itself.
Oprah Winfrey

Life is full of unexpected and certainly unwanted twists and turns, but what makes us who we are is determined by the way we handle those situations. This is what separates us from those who achieve and those who allow others to control their fate.
Jennifer Cruz

Every great dream begins with a dreamer. Always remember, you have within you the strength, the patience, and the passion to reach for the stars to change the world.
Harriet Tubman

If you don't risk anything you risk even more.
Erica Jong

In the long run, we shape our lives, and we shape ourselves. The process never ends until we die and the choices we make are ultimately our own responsibility.
Eleanor Roosevelt

It is important to use all knowledge ethically, humanely and lovingly.
Carol Pearson

If you can't be a genius, imitate the daring.
Eudora Welty

The person interested in success has to learn to view failure as a healthy, inevitable part of the process of getting to the top.
Dr. Joyce Brothers

If you have love in your life, it can make up for a great many things you lack. If you don't have it, no matter what else there is, it is not enough.
Ann Landers

Mistakes are part of the dues one pays for a full life.
Sophia Loren

Look at a day when you are supremely satisfied at the end. It's not a day when you lounge around doing nothing; it's when you've everything to do, and you've done it.
Margaret Thatcher

To keep our faces toward change, and behave like free spirits in the presence of fate, is strength undefeatable.
Helen Keller

If you try to guard yourself against every unlikely danger, you'll never stretch beyond your comfort zone. Don't let "what-ifs" run your life. Follow your dreams and have at it.
Diane Conway

It is only when we truly know and understand that we have a limited time on Earth and that we have no way of knowing when our time is up that we will begin to live each day to the fullest, as if it were the only one we had.
Elisabeth Kübler-Ross

The young do not know enough to be prudent, and therefore they attempt the impossible — and achieve it, generation after generation.
Pearl S. Buck

I've learned that making a "living" is not the same thing as "making" a life.
Maya Angelou

We are taught you must blame your father, your sisters, your brothers, the school, the teachers — you can blame anyone but never blame yourself — it's never your fault. But it's always your fault, because if you wanted to change, you're the one who has got to change. It's as simple as that, isn't it?
Katharine Hepburn

I must admit that I personally measure success in terms of the contributions an individual makes to their fellow human beings.
Margaret Mead

A woman is like a tea bag. You never know how strong she is until she gets into hot water.
Eleanor Roosevelt

The most painful moral struggles are not those between good and evil, but between the good and the lesser good.
Barbara Grizzuti Harrison

Preconceived notions are the locks on the door to wisdom.
Merry Browne

You find yourself refreshed in the presence of cheerful people. Why not make an honest effort to confer that pleasure on others? Half the battle is gained if you never allow yourself to say anything gloomy.
Lydia M. Child

Creativity is not restricted to the arts. Creativity is an approach to living life.
Alyce Cornyn-Selby

Feel the power that comes from focusing on what excites you.
Oprah Winfrey

What a wonderful life I've had! I only wish I'd realized it sooner.
Sidonie-Gabrielle Colette

We live in the present, we dream of the future, we learn eternal truths from the past.
Madame Chiang Kai-Shek

One of the signs of passing youth is the birth of a sense of fellowship with other human beings as we take our place among them.
Virginia Woolf

When we leave this world, how much we have loved will be our true legacy. It is the only thing we will leave behind and carry with us.
Anne Siloy

I never dreamed about success. I worked for it.
Estée Lauder

If you don't go after what you want, you'll never have it. If you don't ask, the answer is always no. If you don't step forward, you're always in the same place.
Nora Roberts

If your energy is as boundless as your ambition, total commitment may be a way of life you should seriously consider.
Dr. Joyce Brothers

The past is not your potential. In any hour you can choose to liberate the future.
Marilyn Ferguson

You gain strength, courage, and confidence by every experience in which you really stop to look fear in the face. You must do the thing you think you cannot do.
Eleanor Roosevelt

The most pathetic person in the world is someone who has sight, but has no vision.
Helen Keller

To succeed in life, you need three things: a wishbone, a backbone and a funny bone.
Reba McEntire

You can stand tall without standing on someone. You can be a victor without having victims.
Harriet Woods

Giving whether it be of time, labor, affection, advice, gifts, or whatever, is one of life's greatest pleasures.
Rebecca Russell

I am beginning to learn that it is the sweet, simple things of life which are the real ones after all.
Laura Ingalls Wilder

Give without remembering and take without forgetting.
Liz Bebesco

We don't have to wait for fear to vanish altogether because that moment will never come; all we need is a moment of daring that can change a whole lifetime of waiting.
Diane Conway

The two important things I did learn were that you are as powerful and strong as you allow yourself to be, and that the most difficult part of any endeavor is taking the first step, making the first decision.
Robyn Davidson

Some people say I have attitude — maybe I do. But I think you have to. You have to believe in yourself when no one else does — that makes you a winner right there.
Venus Williams

When you cease to make a contribution, you begin to die.
Eleanor Roosevelt

Opportunity is sometimes hard to recognize if you're only looking for a lucky break.
Monta Crane

About the only thing that comes to us without effort is old age.
Gloria Pitzer

Personal action is your pathway to success, even if it is a little bit at a time!
Catherine Pulsifer

In every single thing you do, you are choosing a direction. Your life is a product of choices.
Kathleen Hall

Being defeated is often a temporary condition. Giving up is what makes it permanent.
Marilyn vos Savant

Let the barriers you face —— and there will be barriers —— be external, not internal.
Sheryl Sandberg

Concentrate, play your game, and don't be afraid to win.
Louisa May Alcott

Lots of people want to ride with you in the limo, but what you want is someone who will take the bus with you when the limo breaks down.
Oprah Winfrey

To have character is to be big enough to take life on.
Mary Caroline Richards

Risk! Risk anything! Care no more for the opinion of others, for those other voices. Do the hardest thing on earth for you. Act for yourself. Face the truth.
Katherine Mansfield

Unless your heart, your soul, and your whole being are behind every decision you make, the words from your mouth will be empty, and each action will be meaningless.
Kathleen Pedersen

Only when we are no longer afraid do we begin to live.
Dorothy Thompson

If you find it in your heart to care for somebody else, you will have succeeded.
Maya Angelou

I think the most important thing you can be to someone else is dependable. In this world, it's nice to have a person you can count on!
Julianna Margulies

Character isn't inherited. One builds it daily by the way one thinks and acts, thought by thought, action by action.
Helen Gahagan Douglas

One of the lessons that I grew up with was to always stay true to yourself and never let what somebody says distract you from your goals.
Michelle Obama

To achieve you need thought. You have to know what you are doing and that's real power.
Ayn Rand

It's better to walk alone than with a crowd going in the wrong direction.
Diane Grant

It's important that we're not only confident that we have what it takes to achieve, but that we know when we need help.
Karen R. Koenig

I alone cannot change the world, but I can cast a stone across the waters to create many ripples.
Mother Teresa

You know you are on the road to success if you would do your job and not be paid for it.
Oprah Winfrey

The smartest thing I ever did was to hire my weakness.
Sara Blakely

When we give ourselves permission to fail, we, at the same time, give ourselves permission to excel.
Eloise Ristad

Champions know there are no shortcuts to the top. They climb the mountain one step at a time. They have no use for helicopters.
Judi Adler

With any trial and circumstance, a person's true color either shines or darkens.
Shannon Walker

My private measure of success is daily. If this were to be the last day of my life would I be content with it? To live in a harmonious balance of commitments and pleasures is what I strive for.
Jane Rule

It's how you deal with failure that determines how you achieve success.
Charlotte Whitton

No matter what accomplishments you make, somebody helped you.
Althea Gibson

The essential question is not, "How busy are you?" but "What are you busy at?"
Oprah Winfrey

Do not call procrastination laziness. Call it fear.
Julia Cameron

Women must try to do things as men have tried. When they fail, their failure must be but a challenge to others.
Amelia Earhart

We're here for a reason. I believe a bit of the reason is to throw little torches out to lead people through the dark.
Whoopi Goldberg

When you're that successful, things have a momentum, and at a certain point you can't really tell whether you have created the momentum or it's creating you.
Annie Lennox

Talent is distributed equally around the world. Opportunity is not.
Leila Janah

I attribute my success to this: I never gave or took any excuse.
Florence Nightingale

Never start a business just to make money. Start a business to make a difference.
Marie Forleo

Success is most often achieved by those who don't know that failure is inevitable.
Coco Chanel

It takes a lot of courage to show your dreams to someone else.
Erma Bombeck

If you are successful, it is because somewhere, sometime, someone gave you a life or an idea that started you in the right direction. Remember also that you are indebted to life until you help some less fortunate person, just as you were helped.
Melinda Gates

I do not know anyone who has gotten to the top without hard work. That is the recipe. It will not always get you to the top, but it will get you pretty near.
Margaret Thatcher

To be successful, you don't have to change who you are; you have to become more of who you are.
Sally Hogshead

The weak fall, but the strong will remain and never go under!
Anne Frank

Sometimes you don't realize your own strength until you come face to face with your greatest weakness.
Susan Gale

If you are never scared, embarrassed or hurt, it means you never take chances.
Julia Soul

Real courage is when you know you're licked before you begin, but you begin anyway and see it through no matter what.
Harper Lee

Luck can only get you so far.
J. K. Rowling

If you have made mistakes, there is always another chance for you. You may have a fresh start any moment you choose. For this thing we call "Failure" is not the falling down, but the staying down.
Mary Pickford

There is natural talent, but not overnight success.
Patricia Fripp

My philosophy is that not only are you responsible for your life, but doing the best at this moment puts you in the best place for the next moment.
Oprah Winfrey

Success is a great deodorant.
Elizabeth Taylor

I beg you take courage; the brave soul can mend even disaster.
Catherine the Great

Sometimes things have to go wrong in order to go right.
Sherrilyn Kenyon

Your opponent, in the end, is never really the player on the other side of the net, or the swimmer in the next lane, or the team on the other side of the field, or even the bar you must high jump. Your opponent is yourself, your negative internal voices, your level of determination.
Grace Lichtenstein

Strength isn't about bearing a cross of grief or shame. Strength comes from choosing your own path, and living with the consequences.
Jenny Trout

If you want to feel good, you have to go out and do some good.
Oprah Winfrey

Great difficulties may be surmounted by patience and perseverance.
Abigail Adams

We call our little girls bossy. Go to a playground; little girls get called bossy all the time — a word that's almost never used for boys — and that leads directly to the problems women face in the workforce.
Sheryl Sandberg

Use what you've been through as fuel, believe in yourself and be unstoppable!
Yvonne Pierre

Rock bottom became the solid foundation on which I rebuilt my life.
J. K. Rowling

Defeat is simply a signal to press onward.
Helen Keller

What does it take to be a champion? Desire, dedication, determination, concentration and the will to win.
Patty Berg

The ladder of success is the best climbed by stepping on the rungs of opportunity.
Ayn Rand

If you're presenting yourself with confidence, you can pull off pretty much anything.
Katy Perry

Tiny steps make the big steps happen. Never let a small accomplishment go by without praising yourself to the hilt.
Karen R. Koenig

Women, like men, should try to do the impossible. And when they fail, their failure should be a challenge to others.
Amelia Earhart

Find something that makes you happy and go for it.
Zendaya

I've learned that success comes in a very prickly package. Whether you choose to accept it or not is up to you. It's what you choose to do with it, the people you choose to surround yourself with. Always choose people that are better than you. Always choose people that challenge you and are smarter than you. Always be the student. Once you find yourself to be the teacher, you've lost it.
Sandra Bullock

Think like a queen. A queen is not afraid to fail. Failure is another stepping stone to greatness.
Oprah Winfrey

Define success on your own terms, achieve it by your own rules, and build a life you're proud to live.
Anne Sweeney

Sometimes knowing when to give up is the real test of character.
Susan Elizabeth Phillips

What makes life dreary is the want of a motive.
Mary Ann Evans

No country can ever truly flourish if it stifles the potential of its women and deprives itself of the contributions of half of its citizens.
Michelle Obama

It's time to let go of the frozen, stagnant ideals of traditional success.
Michele Riley Swiderski

Successful people do what others know they should do but will not. To become a success, or just be more successful, you will do what average, less-motivated people will not.
Chalene Johnson

Success is liking yourself, liking what you do, and liking how you do it.
Maya Angelou

The road to success is always under construction.
Lily Tomlin

Stand often in the company of dreamers: they prickle your common sense and believe you can achieve things which are impossible.
Mary Anne Radmacher

I ask not for any crown, but that which all may win; Nor try to conquer any world except the one within.
Louisa May Alcott

The problem with people is they forget that most of the time it's the small things that count.
Jennifer Niven

If you doubt you can accomplish something, then you can't accomplish it. You have to have confidence in your ability, and then be tough enough to follow through.
Rosalyn Carter

On small crack does not mean that you are broken; it means you were put to the test and you didn't fall apart.
Linda Poindexter

It's choice — not chance — that determines your destiny.
Jean Nidetch

The big secret in life is there is no secret. Whatever your goal. You can get there if you're willing to work.
Oprah Winfrey

Sometimes, when we're not looking for what we want, we find what we need.
Erin Loechne

Sometimes the best helping hand you can get is a good, firm push.
Joann Thomas

Anything's possible if you've got enough nerve.
J. K. Rowling

Extraordinary people visualize not what is possible or probable, but rather what is impossible. And by visualizing the impossible, they begin to see it as possible.
Chérie Carter-Scott

If you can't do it for yourself, you do it for all the other young souls who need to be shown that things are possible. That they too can do that thing they dream of.
Charlotte Eriksson

Doubt kills more dreams than failure ever will.
Suzy Kassem

Idealists foolish enough to throw caution to the winds have advanced mankind and have enriched the world.
Emma Goldman

I believe the most important single thing, beyond discipline and creativity, is daring to dare.
Maya Angelou

The length of time it takes to reach your goal depends on the intensity of your desire.
Michelle C. Ustaszewski

Don't try to figure out what other people want to hear from you; figure out what you have to say. It's the one and only thing you have to offer.
Barbara Kingsolver

Having an authentic purpose is becoming an increasing source of competitive advantage.
Rebecca Henderson

We must believe that we are gifted for something, and that this thing, at whatever cost, must be attained.
Marie Curie

Celebrate what you've accomplished but raise the bar a little higher each time you succeed.
Mia Hamm

Success isn't about how much money you make. It's about the difference you make in people's lives.
Michelle Obama

Luck is not chance, it's toil; fortune's expensive smile is earned.
Emily Dickinson

The trick is to listen to your instinct, grab the opportunity when it presents itself and then give it your all. You will stumble and fall, you will experience both disaster and triumph, sometimes in the same day, but it's really important to remember that like a hangover, neither triumphs nor disasters last forever. They both pass and a new day arrives. Just try to make that new day count.
Helen Mirren

Lean forward into your life. Begin each day as if it were on purpose.
Mary Ann Radmacher

My mother drew a distinction between achievement and success. She said that achievement is the knowledge that you have studied and worked hard and done the best that is within you. Success is being praised by others. That is nice but not as important or satisfying. Always aim for achievement and forget about success.
Helen Hayes

You could certainly say that I've never underestimated myself, there's nothing wrong with being ambitious.
Angela Merkel

Power is not given to you. You have to take it.
Beyoncé

A lot of people are afraid to say what they want. That's why they don't get what they want.
Madonna

My dad encouraged us to fail. Growing up, he would ask us what we failed at that week. If we didn't have something, he would be disappointed. It changed my mindset at an early age that failure is not the outcome, failure is not trying. Don't be afraid to fail.
Sara Blakely

Think of all the achievements in your life and how much you know now that you didn't before you started down the road to success.
Karen R. Koenig

I believe you never should spend your time being the former anything.
Condoleezza Rice

If you want to get to the top in life, you are going to have to take the stairs.
Michelle C. Ustaszewski

All serious daring starts from within.
Eudora Welty

Just try new things. Step out of your comfort zones and soar, all right?
Michelle Obama

Sometimes, what you're looking for is already there.
Aretha Franklin

Change your thoughts from "What's in it for me?" to "How can I help?" This is one of the keys to success.
Catherine Pulsifer

Be less curious about people and more curious about ideas.
Marie Curie

You create opportunities by performing, not complaining.
Muriel Siebert

Being a successful person is not necessarily defined by what you have achieved, but by what you have overcome.
Fannie Flagg

The way to achieve your own success is to be willing to help somebody else get it first.
Iyanla Vanzant

We think, mistakenly, that success is the result of the amount of time we put in at work, instead of the quality of time we put in.
Ariana Huffington

Someone once told me growth and comfort do not coexist. And I think it's a really good thing to remember.
Ginni Rometty

Hard work keeps the wrinkles out of the mind and spirit.
Helena Rubinstein

If you don't see a clear path for what you want, sometimes you have to make it yourself.
Mindy Kaling

I want anyone who is looking up to me to see no shame — only pride.
Samira Wiley

We must resist. We must refuse to disappear.
Margaret Atwood

Our lives are fashioned by our choices. First, we make our choices. Then our choices make us.
Anne Frank

Define success on your own terms, achieve it by your own rules, and build a life you're proud to live.
Anne Sweeney

I used to walk down the street like I was a super star. I want people to walk around delusional about how great they can be — and then to fight so hard for it every day that the lie becomes the truth.
Lady Gaga

The only way to do something in depth is to work hard. The moment you start being in love with what you're doing, and thinking it's beautiful or rich, then you're in danger.
Miuccia Prada

I didn't know what I wanted to do, but I always knew the woman I wanted to be.
Diane Von Furstenberg

When you're building a business, you're either all in, or you're not.
Barbara Corcoran

Don't waste a single second. Just move forward as fast as you can, and go for it.
Rebecca Woodcock

CHAPTER 6

Achieving Results

Adriana

There must be a constant search to achieve what we pursue in life. If we do not get the results we are hoping for, we must change the strategy and be resourceful, creative, persevering, and disciplined to finally achieve success. Sometimes the road can be long, heavy, and uphill, but this route is and will be part of the great enjoyment when the desired goal is achieved.

Failures appear when we expect immediate results, we stop believing in ourselves, we fail to overcome failures, we avoid change, we focus on weaknesses, we feel we do not deserve success, and when we do not believe it can be possible. Stay the course; fight to the end and you will win.

The roots of true achievement lie in the will to become the best you can be.

Steven

As I wrote earlier, the art of great leadership focuses on attaining progress. Even if desired results are not attained, achieving progress moves you in the right direction and sets you up for future success.

The best results come when you enjoy what you do, concentration and focus put you into flow, and you are doing something meaningful for yourself or others. You gain authentic satisfaction and happiness by reaching your full potential.

Being self-driven also requires taking responsibility for the outcomes of the actions you take, both good and bad. You, and you alone, are responsible for the energy and attitude you bring into every situation you face and every interaction with other people.

Your energy and your attitude influence the results you will achieve. Your life is in your hands. It is up to you to determine your happiness, your satisfaction, and your contentment. No one else gets the credit or the blame.

Challenge everything you do.
Expand your thinking.
Refocus your efforts.
Rededicate yourself to your future.

Patricia Fripp

Achieving Results
Quotes

There are no shortcuts to any place worth going.
Beverly Sills

A mediocre idea that generates enthusiasm will go further than a great idea that inspires no one.
Mary Kay Ash

I was taught that the way of progress was neither swift nor easy.
Marie Curie

Challenge everything you do. Expand your thinking. Refocus your efforts. Rededicate yourself to your future.
Patricia Fripp

If I work on a certain move constantly, then finally, it doesn't seem risky to me. The idea is that the move stays dangerous and it looks dangerous to my foes, but it is not to me. Hard work has made it easy.
Nadia Comăneci

When nothing is sure, everything is possible.
Margaret Drabble

It is more important to know where you are going than to get there quickly.
Mabel Newcomber

The cure for boredom is curiosity. There is no cure for curiosity.
Ellen Parr

The lowest common denominator is never a high standard.
Jessica Hagy

You can't always expect a certain result, but you can expect to do your best.
Anita Hill

Think big, start small.
Patricia Fripp

Sometimes good things fall apart, so better things can fall together.
Marilyn Monroe

When we tire of well-worn ways, we seek for new. This restless craving in the souls of men spurs them to climb, and to seek the mountain view.
Ella Wheeler Wilcox

One accurate measurement is worth a thousand expert opinions.
Admiral Grace Murray Hopper

The world is moved not only by the mighty shoves of the heroes, but also by the aggregate of the tiny pushes of each honest worker.
Helen Keller

Your work comes only moment by moment.
Priscilla Maurice

We first must think "I can," then behave appropriately along that line of thought.
Marsha Sinetar

The distance is nothing; it is only the first step that is difficult.
Madame Marie du Deffand

It is a common delusion that you can make things better by talking about them.
Rose Macaulay

The true order of learning should be: first, what is necessary; second, what is useful; and third, what is ornamental. To reverse this arrangement is like beginning to build at the top of the edifice.
Lydia Sigourney

Don't follow the crowd, let the crowd follow you.
Margaret Thatcher

Nothing kills a good idea like a committee.
Jessica Hagy

While they were saying among themselves "it cannot be done," it was done.
Helen Keller

If we would have new knowledge, we must get us a whole world of new questions.
Susanne K. Langer

I long to accomplish a great and noble task, but it is my chief duty to accomplish small tasks as if they were great and noble.
Helen Adams Keller

Decide on what you think is right, and stick to it.
Mary Ann Evans

Advances are made by those with at least a touch of irrational confidence in what they can do.
Joan L. Curcio

Great thoughts speak only to the thoughtful mind, but great actions speak to all mankind.
Emily P. Bissell

It's been said that there are two days over which we have no control: yesterday, because it's a cancelled check, and tomorrow, because it's a promissory note.
Diane Conway

Great minds discuss idea, average minds discuss events, small minds discuss people.
Eleanor Roosevelt

If you do something with your whole heart and it's a mistake, you can live with that.
Florence Welch

To think too long about doing a thing often becomes its undoing.
Eva Young

Nothing is more revealing than movement.
Martha Graham

A problem clearly stated is a problem half solved.
Dorothea Brande

Stay away from what might have been and look at what will be.
Marsha Petrie Sue

Nothing destroys a good idea faster than a mandatory consensus.
Jessica Hagy

Have a bias toward action. Let's see something happen now. You can break that big plan into small steps and take the first step right way.
Indira Gandhi

In chaos, there is fertility.
Anaïs Nin

Creativity is inventing, experimenting, growing, taking risks, breaking rules, making mistakes, and having fun.
Mary Lou Cook

The most difficult thing is the decision to act, the rest is merely tenacity.
Amelia Earhart

Can anything be sadder than work left unfinished? Yes, work never begun.
Christina Rossetti

I can do things you cannot, you can do things I cannot; together we can do great things.
Mother Teresa

Decide...whether or not the goal is worth the risks involved. If it is, stop worrying.
Amelia Earhart

Motivation comes from working on things we care about. It also comes from working with people we care about.
Sheryl Sandberg

Passion is energy. Feel the power that comes from focusing on what excites you.
Oprah Winfrey

Don't confuse progress with winning.
Mary Barra

If you just set out to be liked, you will be prepared to compromise on anything at any time, and would achieve nothing.
Margaret Thatcher

We are not interested in the possibilities of defeat; they do not exist.
Queen Victoria

What looks like multitasking is really switching back and forth between multiple tasks, which reduces productivity and increases mistakes by up to 50 percent.
Susan Cain

Growth and comfort do not coexist. That's true for people, companies, and nations.
Ginni Rometty

One part at a time, one day at a time, we can accomplish any goal we set for ourselves.
Karen Casey

Trust the still, small voice that says, "this might work and I'll try it."
Diane Mariechild

The future belongs to charismatic communicators who are technically competent.
Patricia Fripp

When you play it too safe, you're taking the biggest risk of your life. Time is the only wealth we're given.
Barbara Sher

The most effective way to do it, is to do it.
Amelia Earhart

I think one's feelings waste themselves in words; they ought all to be distilled into actions which bring results.
Florence Nightingale

Regardless of how you feel inside, always try to look like a winner. Even if you are behind, a sustained look of control and confidence can give you a mental edge that results in victory.
Diane Arbus

To be disciplined is to follow in a good way. To be self-disciplined is to follow in a better way.
Corita Kent

Over the long run, the unglamorous habit of frequency fosters both productivity and creativity.
Gretchen Rubin

Productivity growth, however it occurs, has a disruptive side to it. In the short term, most things that contribute to productivity growth are very painful.
Janet Yellen

Life is too complicated not to be orderly.
Martha Stewart

If it's worth doing, it's worth overdoing.
Ayn Rand

If you have time to whine then you have time to find a solution.
Dee Dee Artner

The key to productivity is to rotate your avoidance techniques.
Shannon Wheeler

It's very hard to have ideas. It's very hard to put yourself out there, it's very hard to be vulnerable, but those people who do that are the dreamers, the thinkers and the creators. They are the magic people of the world.
Amy Poehler

Your dream will never let you rest, it will keep knocking at your mind's door in still imagination which will lead to a creative mind. Let loose your imagination and begin to create everything that's given to you before the foundations of the earth. Dream like never before.
Euginia Herlihy

It is the possibility of the dream, which quickens my spirit to take action.
Lailah Gifty Akita

Every dream is the beginning of a new life in your thoughts.
Munia Khan

An idea is only as good as how well you can execute it.
Kim Perell

Don't let the walls fall down and crash your dreams. Build more walls up as you succeed.
Laci Midgley

No one has ever achieved anything from the smallest to the greatest unless the dream was dreamed first.
Laura Ingalls Wilder

Reach high, for stars lie hidden in your soul. Dream deep, for every dream precedes the goals.
Pamela Vaull Starr

If you don't value your time, neither will others. Stop giving away your time and talents. Value what you know and start charging for it.
Kim Garst

My confidence comes from the daily grind — training my butt off day in and day out.
Hope Solo

When action grows unprofitable, gather information; when information grows unprofitable, sleep.
Ursula Kroeber Le Guin

Standing in the middle of the road is very dangerous; you get knocked down by the traffic from both sides.
Margaret Thatcher

You have enough to create what you want.
Lailah Gifty Akita

I learned the value of hard work by working hard.
Margaret Mead

There are two kinds of people, those who do the work and those who take the credit. Try to be in the first group; there is less competition there.
Indira Gandhi

It is not hard work which is dreary; it is superficial work.
Edith Hamilton

One never notices what has been done; one can only see what remains to be done.
Marie Curie

You get nothing done if you don't listen to each other.
Barbara Bush

Your dreams create higher foundations. Establish your route and begin climbing.
Michelle C. Ustaszewski

Don't spend time beating on a wall, hoping to transform it into a door.
Coco Chanel

Do not check your soul at the door when you cross the threshold of your workplace. Whether you are a custodian or a CEO, practice work as sacred art. Respect comes not from the work you do, but the way you do your work.
Mary Morrissey

Only surround yourself with people who will lift you higher.
Oprah Winfrey

Achieving a goal provides immediate satisfaction; the process of achieving a goal is a lasting pleasure.
Evelyn Berezin

You can only become great at that thing you're willing to sacrifice for.
Maya Angelou

Done is better than perfect.
Sheryl Sandberg

Persistence penetrates.
Michelle C. Ustaszewski

Do not seek for information of which you can make no use.
Anna Brackett

Whatever you want to do, if you want to be great at it, you have to love it and be able to make sacrifices for it.
Maya Angelou

But you have to do what you dream of doing even while you're afraid.
Arianna Huffington

You may be disappointed if you fail, but you are doomed if you don't try.
Beverly Sills

You don't make progress by standing on the sidelines, whimpering and complaining. You make progress by implementing ideas.
Shirley Chisholm

Alone we can do so little; together we can do so much.
Helen Keller

Allow your dream to start from the lowest level, let it develop and let it grow in a reasonable pace because there is no room for cutting corners.
Euginia Herlihy

None of us, including me, ever do great things. But we can all do small things, with great love, and together we can do something wonderful.
Mother Teresa

The secret of joy in work is contained in one word — excellence. To know how to do something well is to enjoy it.
Pearl S. Buck

Goals give us direction. They put a powerful force into pay on a universal, conscious, and subconscious level. Goals give our life direction.
Melody Beattie

I didn't get there by wishing for it or hoping for it, but by working for it.
Estée Lauder

You can waste your lives drawing lines. Or you can live your life crossing them.
Shonda Rhimes

There's rarely a straight path to something you want to be or do.
Vicky Booth

I believe that if you'll just stand up and go, life will open up for you.
Tina Turner

Act boldly and unseen forces will come to your aid.
Dorothy Brande

To have a dream is a do or die so you have to persuade it with patience; you must have a room for challenges and a room for criticisms.
Euginia Herlihy

Trying to do it all and expecting that it all can be done exactly right is a recipe for disappointment. Perfection is the enemy.
Sheryl Sandberg

Our emerging workforce is not interested in command-and-control leadership. They don't want to do things because I said so, they want to do things because they want to do them.
Irene Rosenfield

Find the smartest people you can and surround yourself with them.
Marissa Meyer

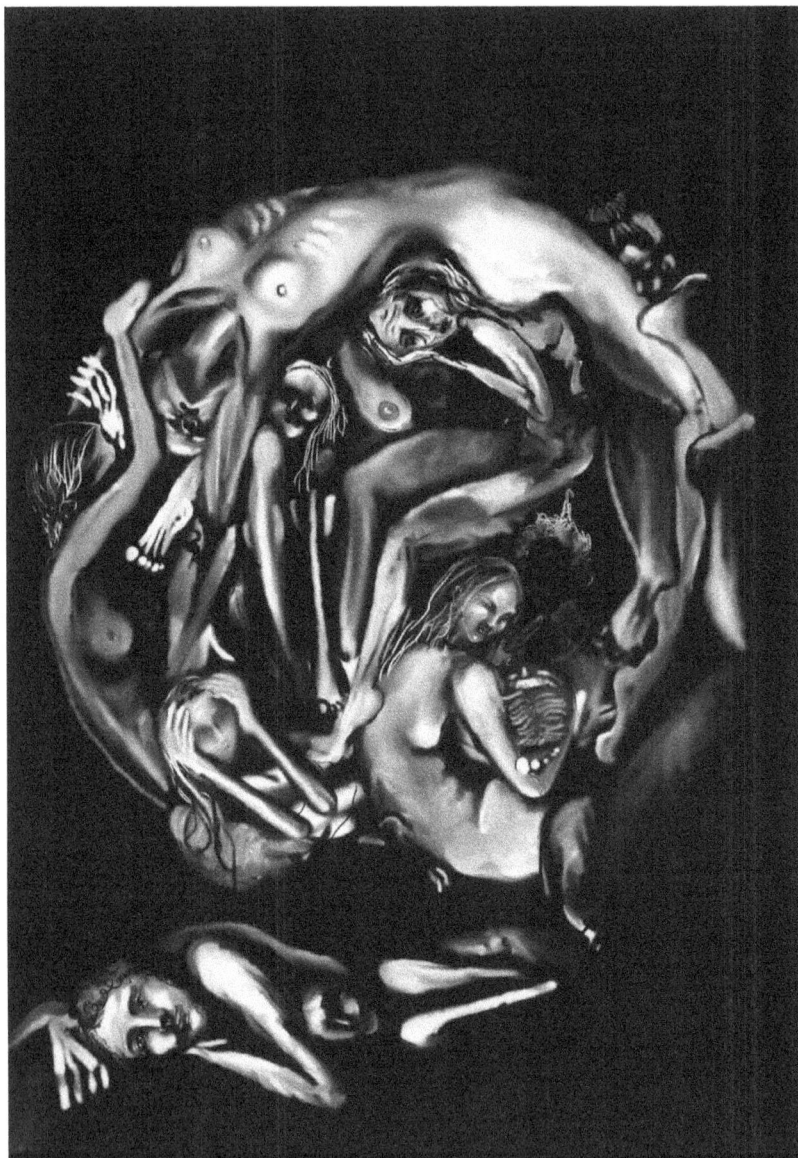

CHAPTER 7

Challenges and Setbacks

Adriana

You must face any challenge from an optimistic perspective, a positive vision, and thinking that everything will be fine and that achieving a goal will only be a matter of time. It may take a bit more effort, but it just means you have to try harder to attain it. Above all, if fate tells you "no" at first, you should keep fighting.

There are times when everything seems to go wrong. Nothing turns out as you expect. Things get tangled and do not arrive, or arrive at the wrong time. Nothing is consolidated. Everything is confusing. And you can feel that you are exhausted, that there is nothing left within to face the difficulties.

These losing streaks often alter our perspective on events. We become more sensitive to everything negative and can easily fall into a pit of pessimism. It is in these moments that we must remember five great truths that we sometimes overlook: 1) everything happens for a reason, 2) pain is a source of growth, 3) complaining and worrying never helps, 4) patience does work, and 5) to always keep going is better than stopping or standing still.

Steven

Commitment is dedication. Persistence is the determination to see something through to the end, not quitting when obstacles appear or the going gets tough.

Often when you read about successful people you learn that they faced times and situations where they wanted to give up, chuck it all in, and move onto something else. Yet something kept them going — a persistence driven by either an internal flame of commitment or an external source of motivation. Such persistence is what frequently separates the successful from those who are not.

Persistence means overcoming failures and turning these into learning experiences. All situations in life can teach us something, particularly the ones we label failures and setbacks. Failure should always be our instructor, not our emotional jailor.

Remember, just as one solitary success does not make you a successful person, one letdown or setback does not make you a failure. No matter how many attempts it takes you to achieve a dream or a goal, as long as you exude continuous persistence in pursuit of your desires you will attain success in your life.

By cultivating gratitude, you eventually expand your internal sense of what is possible, regardless of seeming obstacles and challenges you go through.

Veronica Smith

Challenges and Setbacks Quotes

It is not in the still calm of life, or the repose of a pacific station, that great characters are formed. The habits of a vigorous mind are formed in contending with difficulties.
Abigail Adams

The key to life is accepting challenges. Once someone stops doing this, he's dead.
Bette Davis

If you are facing a new challenge or being asked to do something that you have never done before don't be afraid to step out. You have more capability than you think you do but you will never see it unless you place a demand on yourself for more.
Joyce Meyer

Believe in yourself, trust your gut, surround yourself with resilient people who inspire you to be better and work hard.
Monique Hicks

If you compared your troubles, or challenges, with those of others, you would surely find that there are those whose troubles make yours look like minor inconveniences.
Catherine Pulsifer

When you take risks you learn that there will be times when you succeed and there will be times when you fail, and both are equally important.
Ellen DeGeneres

A life filled with vicissitudes, uncertainty and hard lessons provides us with skills to better approach new challenges that come along.
Vivian Eisenecher

Challenges are an opportunity to test you and rise to the next level.
Angelica Montrose

You need to have self-esteem to be able to adequately tackle the challenges that life throws at you.
Minka Ferguson

The opportunity to develop resilience comes through difficult circumstances that both highlight and challenge existing mindsets.
Devra Davis

What we choose to do on a daily basis prepares us for the greater things God has in store; those faith challenges that will take us into our promised land.
Lisa Cook

We all find ourselves at times in situations that seem hopeless. And, we all have the choice to do nothing or take action.
Catherine Pulsifer

Noble and great. Courageous and determined. Faithful and fearless. That is who you are and who you have always been. And understanding it can change your life, because this knowledge carries a confidence that cannot be duplicated any other way.
Sheri L. Dew

You can't outwit fate by standing on the sidelines placing little side bets about the outcome of life. Either you wade in and risk everything you have to play the game or you don't play at all. And if you don't play you can't win.
Judith McNaught

Do the one thing you think you cannot do. Fail at it. Try again. Do better the second time. The only people who never tumble are those who never mount the high wire. This is your moment. Own it.
Oprah Winfrey

You never find yourself until you face the truth.
Pearl Bailey

Hard work keeps the wrinkles out of the mind and spirt.
Helena Rubinstein

Next time life's GPS sends you astray, take a deep breath, hold on tight and get ready for the ride.
Michelle Sutter

Resilience is merely putting one foot in front of the other to keep moving — in spite of your fears.
Jennifer Pestikas

Every choice makes a difference as we get ourselves unstuck and move toward the life we desire. Select your choices wisely.
Angie Engstrom

Fear doesn't shut you down; it wakes you up.
Veronica Roth

Resilience is the willingness to not quit, to challenge your habits, and to stay determined to make a difference — first for yourself and then for the rest of the world.
Jackie Simmons

God not only uses our trials to better equip us to help others, he also brings us the right people at the right time with the right resources so that our impact in the world will be greater.
La Tanya Hinton

There are no hopeless situations, only those who have grown helpless about them.
Clare Boothe Luce

Whenever there is chaos, it creates wonderful thinking. I consider chaos a gift.
Septima Poinsette Clark

You will succeed if you persevere, and you will find a joy in overcoming obstacles, a delight in climbing rugged paths, which you would perhaps never know if you did not sometime slip backward.
Helen Keller

When you reach an obstacle, turn it into an opportunity. You have the choice. You can overcome and be a winner, or you can allow it to overcome you and be a loser. The choice is yours and yours alone. Refuse to throw in the towel. Go that extra mile that failures refuse to travel. It is far better to be exhausted from success than to be rested from failure.
Mary Kay Ash

I don't focus on what I'm up against. I focus on my goals and I try to ignore the rest.
Venus Williams

Look at the problems in your life. Ask yourself, "What kind of thoughts am I having that create this?"
Louise L. Hay

It is not in the still calm of life or the repose of a pacific station that great characters are formed. The habits of a vigorous mind are formed in contending with difficulties.
Abigail Adams

Always continue the climb. It is possible for you to do whatever you choose, if you first get to know who you are and are willing to work with a power that is greater than ourselves to do it.
Ella Wheeler Wilcox

When life seems hard, the courageous do not lie down and accept defeat; instead, they are all the more determined to struggle for a better future.
Queen Elizabeth II

The only difference between stumbling blocks and stepping stones is the way in which we use them.
Adriana Doyle

There are moments...brief, shining moments, when the impossible becomes possible.
Kelly Keaton

All things are possible until they are proved impossible and even the impossible may only be so, as of now.
Pearl S. Buck

You may not control all the events that happen to you, but you can decide not to be reduced by them.
Maya Angelou

There's no great loss without some small gain.
Laura Ingalls Wilder

Nothing, I am sure, calls forth the faculties so much as the being obliged to struggle with the world.
Mary Wollstonecraft Shelley

Freedom is a personal and lonely battle. One faces down fears of today so that those of tomorrow might be engaged.
Alice Walker

When you come to a roadblock, take a detour.
Barbara Bush

I have had a lot of setbacks that I have learned from.
Susan Wojcicki

The most important things you will need to know will be taught at Life's University.
Michelle C. Ustaszewski

Creativity comes from trust. Trust your instincts, and never hope more than you work.
Rita Mae Brown

Expecting life to treat you well because you are a good person is like expecting an angry bull not to charge because you are a vegetarian.
Shari Barr

You should never view your challenges as a disadvantage. Instead, it's important for you to understand that your experience facing and overcoming adversity is actually one of your biggest advantages.
Michelle Obama

Tests are a gift. And great tests are a great gift. To fail the test is a misfortune. But to refuse the test is to refuse the gift, and something worse, more irrevocable, than misfortune.
Lois McMaster Bujold

When you take risks, you learn that there will be times when you succeed and there will be times when you fail and both are equally important.
Ellen DeGeneres

Optimism is the faith that leads to achievement. Nothing can be done without hope and confidence.
Helen Keller

Stay afraid, but do it anyway. What's important is the action. You don't have to wait to be confident. Just do it and eventually the confidence will follow.
Carrie Fisher

Fearlessness is like a muscle. I know from my own life that the more I exercise it, the more natural it becomes to not let my fears run me.
Arianna Huffington

Be of good cheer. Do not think of today's failures, but of the success that may come tomorrow. You have set yourselves a difficult task, but you will succeed if you persevere; and you will find a joy in overcoming obstacles.
Helen Keller

If you can push through that feeling of taking a risk, really amazing things can happen.
Marissa Mayer

I don't believe in failure. It is not failure if you enjoyed the process.
Oprah Winfrey

Life is not about how fast you run or how high you climb, but how well you bounce.
Vivian Komori

When life is too easy for us, we must beware or we may not be ready to meet the blows which sooner or later come to everyone, rich or poor.
Eleanor Roosevelt

When life seems hard, the courageous do not lie down and accept defeat. Instead, they are all the more determined to struggle for a better future.
Queen Elizabeth II

Just because you fail once doesn't mean you're gonna fail at everything.
Marilyn Monroe

Failure isn't the end of the road. It's a big red flag saying to you, "Wrong way. Turn around."
Oprah Winfrey

Challenges are opportunities requesting action.
Mari L. McCarthy

Keep walking through the storm. Your rainbow is waiting on the other side.
Heather Stillufsen

We don't develop courage by being happy every day. We develop it by surviving difficult times and challenging adversity.
Barbara De Angelis

You forgive yourself for every failure because you are trying to do the right thing. God knows that and you know it. Nobody else may know it.
Maya Angelou

Trouble is a part of your life, and if you don't share it, you don't give the person who loves you a chance to love you enough.
Dinah Shore

Only a fool confuses fate with destiny. Fate is what happens to us. Destiny is what we make in spite of our fate.
Annie Walker

Change obstacles into challenges. You might have to step back and go a different direction, but you can achieve.
Raye Montague

It's okay — in fact it's better than okay — to make mistakes, really big mistakes sometimes. That strikes me as where all the good stuff happens.
Melissa Harris-Perry

In our lifetime, we meet many types of people. The ones that stand out for me are the ones who overcome challenges and have a positive outlook on life.
Catherine Pulsifer

It is tough to be a trailblazer and to be on the front end on a regular, ongoing basis, but somebody's got to do it.
Marsha Blackburn

You can choose courage, or you can choose comfort, but you cannot choose both.
Brené Brown

If you want something and you've never had it before, you're going to have to do something you've never done before in order to get it.
Tiffany Dufu

We may encounter many defeats, but we must not be defeated. It may even be necessary to encounter the defeat so that we can know who we are. So that we can see, "oh, that happened and I rose. I did get knocked down flat in front of the whole world, and I rose. I didn't run away. I rose right where I'd been knocked down."
Maya Angelou

None of us can know what we are capable of until we are tested.
Elizabeth Blackwell

I like the idea of showing that you can go through a lot and still be on your feet, still be working, and still be positive about life. And that you can still think that the best thing is around the corner.
Gloria Vanderbilt

When you get into a tight place, and everything goes against you till it seems as if you couldn't hold on a minute longer, never give up then, for that's just the place and time that the tide'll turn.
Harriet Beecher Stowe

The key to life is accepting challenges. Once someone stops doing this, he's dead.
Bette Davis

Life's ups and downs provide windows of opportunity to determine your values and goals. Think of using all obstacles as stepping stones to build the life you want.
Marsha Sinetar

Remember, we all stumble, every one of us. That's why it's a comfort to go hand in hand.
Emily Kimbrough

Pain nourishes courage. You can't be brave if you've only had wonderful things happen to you.
Mary Tyler Moore

Apparent failure may hold in its rough shell the germs of a success that will blossom in time, and bear fruit throughout eternity.
Frances Watkins Harper

Character cannot be developed in ease and quiet. Only through experience of trial and suffering can the soul be strengthened, ambition inspired, and success achieved.
Helen Keller

The most beautiful people we have known are those who have known defeat, known suffering, known struggle, known loss, and have found their way out of the depths. These persons have an appreciation, a sensitivity and an understanding of life that fills them with compassions, gentleness, and a deep loving concern. Beautiful people do not just happen.
Elisabeth Kübler-Ross

If we had no winter, the spring would not be so pleasant; if we did not sometimes taste of adversity, prosperity would not be so welcome.
Anne Bradstreet

Storms make trees take deeper roots.
Dolly Parton

Perseverance is failing 19 times and succeeding the 20th.
Julie Andrews

I think the challenge is to take difficult and painful times and turn them into something beneficial, something that makes you grow.
Michelle Akers

You may encounter many defeats, but you must not be defeated. In fact, it may be necessary to encounter the defeats, so you can know who you are, what you can rise from, how you can still come out of it.
Maya Angelou

A happy life consists not in the absence, but in the mastery of hardships.
Helen Keller

When you have that window of opportunity called a crisis, move as quickly as you can, get as much done as you can. There's a momentum for change that's very compelling.
Anne Mulcahy

Turn your wounds into wisdom.
Oprah Winfrey

Burning desire to be or do something gives us staying power — a reason to get up every morning or to pick ourselves up and start again after a disappointment.
Marsha Sinetar

You're either changing your life or you're not. No waiting for this or that or better weather or other hurdles. Hurdles are the change.
Terri Guillemets

Courage doesn't always roar. Sometimes courage is the quiet voice at the end of the day saying, "I will try again tomorrow."
Mary Anne Radmacher

CHAPTER 8

Living Well

Adriana

This will be highly subjective topic for many. Living well has to with the needs, thoughts, and desires of each person.

For me personally, living well first of all means good health for my family and me. Subsequently, it means having a good a balance between my personal, professional, and family life. When I achieve these conditions, I am positioned to enjoy what I do while contributing, growing, developing, and always learning something new.

Work is important, but so too is living and enjoying the simple and beautiful things that life gives us. Additional components of living well include being able to help those most in need, always seeking to be a simpler, integrated, fair, and collaborative person, and, of course, above all being happy.

Travel, laugh, dance, dreaming, and being able to leave a legacy life that helps to create a better world in the future are truly important aspects of a life well lived.

With regards to the latter, we will all have a chance for living well when we see greater equality between women and men and less gender violence.

Steven

The quote from Marianne Williamson at the front of this book best describes our life's purpose, and the definition of living well: "The purpose of our lives is to give birth to the best which is within us."

Buddha, an individual who gave the purpose of life a great deal of thought, concluded, "Your work is to discover your world and then with all your heart give yourself to it."

Combined, these two quotes form the essence of living well. They move us beyond thinking only of material comforts. We should use financial security as the foundation for our spiritual and personal growth, and to make the world a better place for our children and grandchildren.

Living well is being at peace with the world, the people with whom we interact, and ourselves. Over 2000 years ago, Plato observed that "the unexamined life is not worth living." A deep sense of self-awareness and self-understanding (know thyself!) enables us to create individual foundations for living well.

Doing so also makes us more authentic in our behaviors and actions. This is important, for we each teach better lessons through the way we live our lives than the words we express to others and ourselves.

How wonderful it is that nobody need wait a single moment before starting to improve the world.

Anne Frank

Living Well Quotes

Since you get more joy out of giving joy to others, you should put a good deal of thought into the happiness that you are able to give.
Eleanor Roosevelt

For beautiful eyes, look for the good in others; for beautiful lips, speak only words of kindness; and for poise, walk with the knowledge that you are never alone.
Audrey Hepburn

There can be no happiness if the things we believe in are different from the things we do.
Freya Stark

Love and kindness are never wasted. They always make a difference.
Barbara De Angelis

Living well has something to do with the spirituality of wholeheartedness, of seeing life more as a grace than as a penance, as time to be lived with eager expectation of its goodness, not in dread of its challenges.
Joan Chittister

One's life has value so long as one attributes value to the life of others, by means of love, friendship and compassion.
Simone de Beauvoir

Lighthouses don't go running all over an island looking for boats to save; they just stand there, shining.
Anne Lamott

Imagination is the highest kite one can fly.
Lauren Bacall

I get up in the morning and I really do feel that the world is my oyster, and I start that way, the same as I would if I were preparing to write a song: put a blank piece of paper up on the piano and you go for it.
Lesley Gore

Women's propensity to share confidences is universal. We confirm our reality by sharing.
Barbara Grizzuti Harrison

If we learn to open our hearts, anyone, including the people who drive us crazy, can be our teacher.
Pema Chödrön

Real genius is nothing else but the supernatural virtue of humility in the domain of thought.
Simone Weil

Enthusiasm is contagious. Be a carrier.
Susan Rabin

Good communication is as stimulating as black coffee, and just as hard to sleep after.
Anne Morrow Lindbergh

A bird doesn't sing because it has an answer, it sings because it has a song.
Maya Angelou

Fear is inevitable. I have to accept that, but I cannot allow it to paralyze me.
Isabel Allende

Nothing is impossible, the word itself says "I'm possible!"
Audrey Hepburn

Fortune does favor the bold and you'll never know what you're capable of if you don't try.
Sheryl Sandberg

The future is completely open, and we are writing it moment to moment.
Pema Chödrön

I enjoy life when things are happening. I don't care if it's good things or bad things. That means you're alive.
Joan Rivers

Courage is the price that life exacts for granting peace. The soul that knows it not, knows no release from little things.
Amelia Earhart

Life is very interesting. In the end, some of your greatest pains become your greatest strengths.
Drew Barrymore

In order to experience everyday spirituality, we need to remember that we are spiritual beings spending some time in a human body.
Barbara De Angelis

How wonderful it is that nobody need wait a single moment before starting to improve the world.
Anne Frank

Be thankful for what you have; you'll end up having more. If you concentrate on what you don't have, you will never, ever have enough.
Oprah Winfrey

Silent gratitude isn't very much to anyone.
Gertrude Stein

It is impossible to feel grateful and depressed in the same moment.
Naomi Williams

One can never pay in gratitude; one can only pay "in kind" somewhere else in life.
Anne Morrow Lindbergh

If you have a goal in life that takes a lot of energy, that requires a lot of work, that incurs a great deal of interest and that is a challenge to you, you will always look forward to waking up to see what the new day brings.
Susan Polis Schutz

This a wonderful day. I've never seen this one before.
Maya Angelou

Life shrinks or expands I proportion to one's courage.
Anaïs Nin

The biggest adventure you can ever take is to live the life of your dreams.
Oprah Winfrey

You can't use up creativity. The more you use, the more you have.
Maya Angelou

If you trade your authenticity for safety, you may experience the following: anxiety, depression, eating disorders, addiction, rage, blame, resentment, and inexplicable grief.
Brené Brown

Don't wait for your feelings to change to take the action. Take the action and your feelings will change.
Barbara Baron

Happiness is not a goal. It's a by-product of a life well lived.
Eleanor Roosevelt

You are the sum total of everything you've ever seen, heard, eaten, smelled, been told, forgot — it's all there. Everything influences each of us, and because of that I try to make sure that my experiences are positive.
Maya Angelou

In this world of change, nothing which comes stays, nothing which goes is lost.
Anne Sophie Swetchine

Give without remembering, take without forgetting.
Elizabeth Bibesco

If you surrender completely to the moments as they pass, you live more richly those moments.
Anne Morrow Lindbergh

The secret of joy is the mastery of pain.
Anaïs Nin

Never argue with the inevitable.
Patricia Fripp

Courage starts with showing up and letting ourselves be seen.
Brené Brown

Happiness is not a station you arrive at, but a manner of traveling.
Margaret Runbeck

Don't follow any advice, no matter how good, until you feel as deeply in your spirit as you think in your mind that the counsel is wise.
Joan Rivers

Never allow a person to tell you "no" who doesn't have the power to say "yes."
Eleanor Roosevelt

You will discover that you have two hands. One is for helping yourself and the other is for helping others.
Audrey Hepburn

Old age is an excellent time for outrage. My goal is to say or do at least one outrageous thing every week.
Maggie Kuhn

It may be necessary temporarily to accept a lesser evil, but one must never label a necessary evil as good.
Margaret Mead

The future belongs to those who believe in the beauty of their dreams.
Eleanor Roosevelt

Each of us must work for his own improvement, and at the same time share a general responsibility for all humanity.
Marie Curie

You came to this planet to be remarkable.
Victoria Moran

The dream was always running ahead of me. To catch up, to live for a moment in unison with it, that was the miracle.
Anaïs Nin

True compassion does not come from wanting to help out those less fortunate than ourselves but from realizing our kinship with all beings.
Pema Chödrön

You cannot make yourself feel something you do not feel, but you can make yourself do right in spite of your feelings.
Pearl S. Buck

Sometimes the biggest act of courage is a small one.
Lauren Raffo

How we remember, what we remember and why we remember form the most personal map of our individuality.
Christina Baldwin

The things I needed were boring things like consistency, reliability, enthusiasm. We aren't taught to want these things.
Priya-Alika Elias

What makes you vulnerable makes you beautiful.
Brené Brown

To be rich in friends is to be poor in nothing.
Lilian Whiting

Always aim for achievement, and forget about success.
Helen Hayes

To be fully alive, fully human, and completely awake is to be continually thrown out of the nest.
Pema Chödrön

Freedom is instantaneous the moment we accept things as they are.
Karen Maezen Miller

If you have knowledge, let others light their candles in it.
Margaret Fuller

Life's challenges are not supposed to paralyze you, they're supposed to help you discover who you are.
Bernice Johnson Reagon

People with integrity do what they say they are going to do. Others have excuses.
Laura Schlessinger

Many receive advice, only the wise profit from it.
Harper Lee

When you begin to touch your heart or let your heart be touched, you begin to discover that it's bottomless.
Pema Chödrön

What we know matters but who we are matters more.
Brené Brown

All great artists draw from the same resource: the human heart that tells us that we are all more alike than we are unalike.
Maya Angelou

Everybody's a teacher if you listen.
Doris Roberts

Hope is the feeling that the feeling you have isn't permanent.
Joan Kerr

Good enough is the new perfect.
Becky Beaupre Gillespie

An unhurried sense of time is in itself a sort of wealth.
Bonnie Friedman

Mistakes are part of the dues one pays for a full life.
Sophia Loren

When one door of happiness closes, another opens; but often we look so long at the closed door that we do not see the one which has been opened for us.
Helen Keller

It is the ultimate luxury to combine passion and contribution. It's also a very clear path to happiness.
Sheryl Sandberg

When we grow old, there can only be one regret — not to have given enough of ourselves.
Eleonora Duse

Trust yourself. Create the kind of self that you will be happy to live with all your life. Make the most of yourself by fanning the tiny, inner sparks of possibility into flames of achievement.
Golda Meir

Whatever you want in life, other people are going to want too. Believe in yourself enough to accept the idea that you have an equal right to it.
Diane Sawyer

Speculation and the exploration of ideas beyond what we know with certainty are what lead to progress.
Lisa Randall

I can forgive almost anything. But let me be clear: forgiving and excusing are not the same thing.
Michelle R. Gould

Don't be afraid of death; be afraid of an unlived life. You don't have to live forever; you just have to live.
Natalie Babbitt

My definition of courage is never letting anyone define you.
Jenna Jameson

I have no riches but my thoughts, yet these are wealth enough for me.
Sarah Josepha Hale

When someone tells me "no," it doesn't mean I cannot do it, it simply means I cannot do it with them.
Karen E. Quinones Miller

Don't waste your energy trying to change opinions. Do your thing and don't care if they like it.
Tina Fey

Vulnerability sounds like truth and feels like courage. Truth and courage aren't always comfortable, but they're never weakness.
Brené Brown

You wouldn't worry so much about what others think of you if your realized how seldom they do.
Eleanor Roosevelt

You have to accept whatever comes and the only important thing is that you meet it with courage and with the best that you have to give.
Eleanor Roosevelt

We must believe that we are gifted for something, and that this thing, at whatever cost, must be attained.
Marie Curie

Without courage, we cannot practice any other virtue with consistency. We can't be kind, true, merciful, generous, or honest.
Maya Angelou

Courage is very important. Like a muscle, it is strengthened by use.
Ruth Gordon

In all realms of life, it takes courage to stretch your limits, express your power, and fulfill your potential.
Suze Orman

It is impossible to live without failing at something, unless you live so cautiously that you might as well not have lived at all, in which case you have failed by default.
J. K. Rowling

Holding on is believing that there's only a past; letting go is knowing that there's a future.
Daphne Rose Kingma

There's an important difference between giving up and letting go.
Jessica Hatchigan

You've got to make a conscious choice every day to shed the old — whatever "the old" means for you.
Sarah Ban Breathnach

Authenticity is a collection of choices that we have to make every day. It's about the choice to show up and be real. The choice to be honest. The choice to let our true selves be seen.
Brené Brown

Yesterday is a cancelled check; tomorrow is a promissory note; today is the only cash you have — so spend it wisely.
Kay Lyons

You can clutch the past so tightly to your chest that it leaves your arms too full to embrace the present.
Jan Glidewell

The question is whether or not you choose to disturb the world around you, or if you choose to let it go on as if you had never arrived.
Ann Patchett

There's no such thing as ruining your life. Life's a pretty resilient thing, it turns out.
Sophie Kinsella

Happiness is an inside job. Don't assign anyone else that much power over your life.
Mandy Hale

Resilience is accepting your new reality, even if it's less good than the one you had before. You can fight it, you can do nothing but scream about what you've lost, or you can accept that and try to put together something that's good.
Elizabeth Edwards

Indeed, this life is a test. It is a test of many things — of our convictions and priorities, our faith and our faithfulness, our patience and our resilience, and in the end, our ultimate desires.
Sheri L. Dew

We can each define ambition and progress for ourselves. The goal is to work toward a world where expectations are not set by the stereotypes that hold us back, but by our personal passion, talents, and interests.
Sheryl Sandberg

Gratitude unlocks the fullness of life. It turns what we have into enough, and more. It turns denial into acceptances, chaos to order, confusion to clarity. It can turn a meal into a feast, a house into a home, a stranger into a friend.
Melody Beattie

Whatever we are waiting for — peace of mind, contentment, grace, the inner awareness of simple abundance — it will surely come to us, but only when we are ready to receive it with an open and grateful heart.
Sara Ban Breathnach

Realize that if a door closed, it's because what was behind it wasn't meant for you.
Mandy Hale

I believe that everything happens for a reason. People change so that you can learn to let go, things go wrong so that you appreciate them when they're right, you believe lies so you eventually learn to trust no one but yourself, and sometimes good things fall apart so better things can fall together.
Marilyn Monroe

I trust that everything happens for a reason, even if we are not wise enough to see it.
Oprah Winfrey

One's philosophy is not be expressed in words; it is express in the choices one makes...and the choices we make are ultimately our responsibility.
Eleanor Roosevelt

Staying vulnerable is a risk we have to take if we want to experience connection.
Brené Brown

Self-worth is so vital to your happiness. If you don't feel good about YOU, it's hard to feel good about anything else.
Mandy Hale

You can never meet your potential until you truly learn to love yourself.
Teresa Collins

We are each gifted in a unique and important way. It is our privilege and our adventure to discover our own special light.
Mary Dunbar

We are all on a life long journey and the core of its meaning, the terrible demand of its centrality is forgiving and being forgiven.
Martha Kilpatrick

Self-love is complete forgiveness, acceptance and respect for who you are deep down — all your beautiful and hideous parts included.
Aletheia Luna

Plant your own garden and decorate your own soul, instead of waiting for someone to bring you flowers.
Veronica A. Shoffstall

Spend time understanding who you are, after all the only person you're ever going to truly live with; is yourself.
Nikki Rowe

The best protection any woman can have...is courage.
Elizabeth Cady Stanton

Remember always that you not only have the right to be an individual, you have an obligation to be one.
Eleanor Roosevelt

Gratitude makes sense of our past, brings peace for today and creates a vision for tomorrow.
Melodie Beattie

When you are your own best friend, you don't endlessly seek out relationships, friendships, and validation from the wrong sources because you realize that the only approval and validation you need is your own.
Mandy Hale

So, there's no such thing as work-life balance. There's work, and there's life, and there's no balance.
Sheryl Sandberg

Do not bring people in your life who weigh you down. And trust your instincts...good relationships feel good. They feel right. They don't hurt. They're not painful. That's not just with somebody you want to marry, but it's with the friends that you choose. It's with the people you surround yourselves with.
Michelle Obama

I say that the most liberating thing about beauty is realizing that you are the beholder.
Salma Hayek

I'm intimidated by the fear of being average.
Taylor Swift

If you are lucky enough to find a way of life you love, you have to find the courage to live it.
Bette Davis

You can only become truly accomplished at something you love. Don't make money your goal. Instead, pursue the things you love doing and then do them so well that people can't take their eyes off of you.
Maya Angelou

Many people lose the small joys in the hope for the big happiness.
Pearl S. Buck

There's nothing enlightened about shrinking so that other people won't feel insecure around you.
Marianne Williamson

Owning our story and loving ourselves through that process is the bravest think that we'll ever do.
Brené Brown

Once you get rid of the idea that you must please other people before you please yourself, and you begin to follow your own instincts — only then can you be successful. You become more satisfied, and when you are, other people tend to be satisfied by what you do.
Raquel Welch

I have already settled it for myself, so flattery and criticism go down the same drain and I am quite free.
Georgia O'Keeffe

I am always more interested in what I am about to do than what I have already done.
Rachel Carson

If life were predictable it would cease to be life, and be without flavor.
Eleanor Roosevelt

If we can share our story with someone who responds with empathy and understanding, shame can't survive.
Brené Brown

Find ecstasy in life; the mere sense of living is joy enough.
Emily Dickinson

Sometimes you have to be alone to truly know your worth.
Karen A. Baquiran

The most important thing is to enjoy your life — to be happy — it's all that matters.
Audrey Hepburn

Life is short, and it is up to you to make it sweet.
Sarah Louise Delany

The only real prison is fear, and the only real freedom is freedom from fear.
Aung San Suu Kyi

Do not ruin today with mourning tomorrow.
Catherynne M. Valente

It stands to reason that anyone who learns to live well will die well. The skills are the same: being present in the moment, and humble, and brave, and keeping a sense of humor.
Victoria Moran

There are a thousand thousand reasons to live this life, every one of them sufficient.
Marilynne Robinson

Laugh as much as possible; always laugh. It's the sweetest thing one can do for oneself and one's fellow human beings.
Maya Angelou

Be bold enough to live life on your terms, and never apologize for it.
Mandy Hale

We must have a theme, a goal, a purpose in our lives. If you don't know where you're aiming, you don't have a goal. My goal is to live my life in such a way that when I die, someone can say, "she cared."
Mary Kay Ash

And in life, it is all about choices we make. And how the direction of our lives comes down to the choices we choose.
Catherine Pulsifer

In every single thing you do, you are choosing a direction. Your life is a product of choices.
Dr. Kathleen Hall

Don't be intimidated by what you don't know. That can be your greatest strength and ensure that you do things differently from everyone else.
Sara Blakely

I decided, very early on, just to accept life unconditionally; I never expected it to do anything special for me, yet I seemed to accomplish far more than I had ever hoped. Most of the time it just happened to me without my ever seeking it.
Audrey Hepburn

Don't you dare, for one more second, surround yourself with people who are not aware of the greatness that you are.
Jo Blackwell-Preston

Don't live down to expectations. Go out there and do something remarkable.
Wendy Wasserstein

Honesty and transparency make you vulnerable. Be honest and transparent anyway.
Mother Teresa

Hard times arouse an instinctive desire for authenticity.
Coco Chanel

It's not what you gather but what you scatter that tells what kind of life you've lived.
Helen Walton

We need to find the courage to say no to the things and people that are not serving us if we want to rediscover ourselves and live our lives with authenticity.
Barbara De Angelis

The authentic self is soul made visible.
Sarah Ban Breathnach

Don't settle for a relationship that won't let you be yourself.
Oprah Winfrey

Stepping onto a brand-new path is difficult, but not more difficult than remaining in a situation, which is not nurturing to the whole woman.
Maya Angelou

I've been absolutely terrified every moment of my life and I've never let it keep me from doing a single thing I wanted to do.
Georgia O'Keeffe

Sometimes you just have to regret things and move on.
Charlaine Harris

When a woman becomes her own best friend, life is easier.
Diane von Furstenberg

The day may be approaching when the whole world will recognize woman as the equal of man.
Susan B. Anthony

The greatest act of courage is to be and own all that you are. Without apology. Without excuses and without any masks to cover the truth of who you really are.
Debbie Ford

To be kind to all, to like many and love a few, to be needed and wanted by those we love, is certainly the nearest we can come to happiness.
Mary Stuart

I can be changed by what happens to me. I am not reduced by it.
Maya Angelou

When you lose your ego, you win. It really is that simple.
Shannon L. Alder

Living a successful life is all about stretching yourself. Learning, growing, and then learning some more.
Marly McMillen

The realization that you have control and influence over your own life is a key concept you will need to understand to practice mindfulness.
Janet Louise Stephenson

When you have a dream you've got to grab it and never let go.
Carol Burnett

Real integrity is doing the right thing, knowing that nobody's going to know whether you did it or not.
Oprah Winfrey

The best things in life are free. The second-best things are very, very expensive.
Coco Chanel

Life is not made up of minutes, hours, days, weeks, months, or years, but of moments. You must experience each one before you can appreciate it.
Sarah Ban Breathnach

There is an alchemy in sorrow. It can be transmuted into wisdom, which, if it does not bring joy, can yet bring happiness.
Pearl S. Buck

Ask for what you want and be prepared to get it.
Maya Angelou

Anyone can hide. Facing up to things, working through them, that's what makes you strong.
Sarah Dessen

I have never tried to block out the memories of the past, even though some are painful. I don't understand people who hide from their past. Everything you live through helps to make you the person you are now.
Sophia Loren

The beauty of a woman is not in the clothes she wears, the figure that she carries, or the way she combs her hair. The beauty of a woman is seen in her eyes, because that is the doorway to her heart, the place where love resides.
Audrey Hepburn

Beauty is the shadow of God on the universe.
Gabriela Mistral

Some people think that to be strong is never to feel pain. However, the strongest people are the ones who have felt pain, understood it, accepted it, and learned from it.
Charlotte Dawson

The key to life is accepting challenges. Once someone stops doing this, he's dead.
Bette Davis

Trust yourself. Create the kind of self that you will be happy to live with all your life. Make the most of yourself by fanning the tiny, inner sparks of possibility into flames of achievement.
Golda Meir

What we call our destiny is truly our character and that character can be altered. The knowledge that we are responsible for our actions and attitudes does not need to be discouraging, because it also means that we are free to change this destiny.
Anaïs Nin

The path emerges as you walk it. So simply walk it.
Natasha Allrich

You can learn new things at any time in your life if you're willing to be a beginner. If you actually learn to like being a beginner, the whole world opens up to you.
Barbara Sher

Get comfortable being uncomfortable. That's how you break the plateau and reach the next level.
Chalene Johnson

It is good to have an end to journey toward; but it is the journey that matters, in the end.
Ursula Kroeber Le Guin

Sexiness wears thin after a while and beauty fades, but to be married to a man who makes you laugh every day, ah, now that's a real treat.
Joanne Woodward

Every day we choose who we are by how we define ourselves.
Angelina Jolie

Each person must live their life as a model for others.
Rosa Parks

There will always be a reason why you meet people. Either you need them to change your life or you're the one that will change theirs.
Angel Flonis Harefa

Surrender to what is. Let go of what was. Have faith in what will be.
Sonia Ricotta

Don't confuse having a career with having a life.
Hillary Clinton

Don't live down to expectations. Go out there and do something remarkable.
Wendy Wasserstein

To be tested is good. The challenged life may be the best therapist.
Gail Sheehy

It is confidence in our bodies, minds, and spirits that allows us to keep looking for new adventures.
Oprah Winfrey

Don't let the world tell you who you are, only you get to decide.
Jennifer Truesdale

Talk to yourself like you would to someone you love.
Brené Brown

Be fearless in the pursuit of what sets your soul on fire.
Jennifer Lee

Taking joy in living is a woman's best cosmetic.
Rosalind Russell

Nobody gets to live life backward. Look ahead, that is where your future lies.
Ann Landers

The older I get, the more I'm conscious of ways very small things can make a change in the world. Tiny little things, but the world is made up of tiny matters, isn't it?
Sandra Cisneros

I trust that everything happens for a reason, even if we are not wise enough to see it.
Oprah Winfrey

Do you believe that there are no coincidences in life? Everything happens for a reason. Every person we meet have a roll in our life, either it is big or small. Some will hurt, betray and make us cry. Some will teach us lesson, not to change us, but to make us to be a better person.
Cynthia Rusli

Every minute of every hour of every day you are making the world, just as you are making yourself, and you might as well do it with generosity and kindness and style.
Rebecca Solnit

You cannot get through a single day without having an impact on the world around you. What you do makes a difference, and you have to decide what kind of difference you want to make.
Jane Goodall

Do your little bit of good where you are: it's those little bits of good put together that overwhelm the world.
Karen Duffy

Shine with all you have. When someone tries to blow you out, just take their oxygen and burn brighter.
Katelyn S. Irons

Carve your name on hearts, not tombstones. A legacy is etched into the minds of others and the stories they share about you.
Shannon L. Alder

The most courageous act is still to think for yourself. Aloud.
Coco Chanel

You really didn't see the sadness or the longing unless you already knew it was there. But that was the trick, wasn't it? I always did something I was a little not ready to do. I think that's how you grow. When there's that moment of Wow, I'm not really sure I can do this, and you push through those moments, that's when you have a breakthrough.
Marissa Mayer

If we listened to our intellect, we'd never have a love affair. We'd never have a friendship. We'd never go into business because we'd be too cynical. Well, that's nonsense. You've got to jump off cliffs all the time and build your wings on the way down.
Annie Dillard

Anything truly worth having is well worth the pain or the fear it sometimes takes to it.
Dorci Hill

When we're looking for compassion, we need someone who is deeply rooted, is able to bend and, most of all, embraces us for our strengths and struggles.
Brené Brown

By accepting personal responsibility in life, and showing your scars, you can heal yourself and you excel in business.
Nancy Abramovitz

Live life to the fullest, keep your dreams alive, uplift each other, share a smile and a hug.
Ylona Cavalier

We need four hugs a day for survival. We need eight hugs a day for maintenance. We need 12 hugs a day for growth.
Virginia Satir

Living well is an art that can be developed: a love of life and ability to take great pleasure from small offerings and assurance that the world owes you nothing and that every gift is exactly that, a gift.
Maya Angelou

Life is about making our own choices, our own mistakes, and fighting our own battles. We all deserve to follow our own unique path.
Svietlana Lavrentidi

Second chances are a gift. From them we can help others grow and learn from our mistakes.
Danielle Di Cosola

I don't have to chase extraordinary moments to find happiness, it is right in front of me if I'm paying attention and practicing gratitude.
Brené Brown

Everyone deserves a great life. Amazing things can happen when you step outside of your comfort zone.
Kathy Rosner

Never take a "no" from someone who was never empowered to give you a "yes" in the first place.
Sherry Rauch

Keep a grateful journal. Every night, list five things that you are grateful for. What it will begin to do is change your perspective of your day and your life.
Oprah Winfrey

Dreams are necessary to life.
Anaïs Nin

You can't control the past, but you can control where you do next.
Kirsten Hubbard

While sailing through life, take your good friends along, the scenery will only get better.
Michelle C. Ustaszewski

Positive energy is your priceless life force. Protect it. Don't allow people to draw from your reserves.
Chalene Johnson

The only way your dream will never come true is if you choose not to listen to it.
Michelle Muriel

We are all blessed with different dreams and our duty is to share those dreams with others not envy one another.
Euginia Herlihy

Accomplishment of your dreams requires personal sacrifice and hardworking. May you have a determined spirit, will power and a great passion for the accomplishment of your dreams.
Lailah Gifty Akita

You are worthy of your wildest dreams.
Nicole Guillaume

Life gives us choices. You either grab on with both hands and just go for it, or you sit on the sidelines.
Christine Feehan

Sometimes it's the smallest decisions that can change your life forever.
Keri Russell

Happiness is not a goal; it's a by-product of a life well lived.
Eleanor Roosevelt

You receive from the world what you give to the world.
Oprah Winfrey

If there is something you care about, make a commitment to do something now — starting with today. And choose to live a meaningful and purpose-driven life where you care about people and issues that are much greater than yourself.
Evangeline Mitchell

If you are always trying to be normal, you will never know how amazing you can be.
Maya Angelou

To live is so startling it leaves little times for anything else.
Emily Dickinson

I never did anything according to what anyone else wanted. That's why I think I am happy.
Sandra Bullock

Every day brings a chance for you to draw in a breath, kick off your shoes, and dance.
Oprah Winfrey

There's more to life than being a passenger.
Amelia Earhart

People spend a lifetime searching for happiness; looking for peace. They chase idle dreams, addictions, religions, even other people, hoping to fill the emptiness that plagues them. The irony is the only place they ever needed to search was within.
Ramona L. Anderson

Carry out a random act of kindness, with no expectation of reward, safe in the knowledge that one day someone might do the same for you.
Princess Diana

Dreams pass into the reality of action. From the actions stems the dream again; and this interdependence produces the highest form of living.
Anaïs Nin

With the new day comes new strength and new thoughts.
Eleanor Roosevelt

Your life is an occasion. Rise to it.
Suzanne Weyn

The only thing that makes life possible is permanent, intolerable uncertainty; not knowing what comes next.
Ursula Kroeber Le Guin

There is no greater gift you can give or receive than to honor your calling. It's why you were born. And how you become most truly alive.
Oprah Winfrey

My deepest belief is that to live as if we're dying can set us free. Dying people teach you to pay attention, to forgive and not to sweat the small things.
Anne Lamott

How we spend our days is, of course, how we spend our lives.
Annie Dillard

Leave something good in every day.
Dolly Parton

In times of crisis, we summon up our strength.
Muriel Rukeyser

Never let fear stop you from asking something you don't understand or know. To pretend or to act as if you know is not a wise thing to do.
Catherine Pulsifer

It's important to be willing to make mistakes. The worst that can happen is that you become memorable.
Sara Blakely

Living well is an art that can be developed: a love of life and ability to take great pleasure from small offerings and assurance that the world owes you nothing and that every gift is exactly that, a gift.
Maya Angelou

CHAPTER 9

Wellbeing

Adriana

I personally define health as physical, mental, social, and emotional wellbeing. These aspects are related and go hand-in-hand. Hence, someone with an emotional problem is still sick no matter how well they are physically. To this must be added that health depends entirely on our ability to respond positively to the challenges that life presents us.

Instead of waiting for something extraordinary to happen, we must learn to enjoy the moments and the little things that are part of everyday life. Living better implies doing so in harmony with oneself, with health, and knowing how to prioritize the necessary and important things.

We know that life is often complex, that it brings us things that are beyond our control. But it is up to us to know how to face them with strength, reflection, and always looking for that path that can lead us to happiness.

Put aside what hurts you, stay away from those people who only bring you problems and surround you with their negativity. Fulfill your obligations for the day, but find a moment for yourself where you can let go of anxieties, pressures, and fears.

It is often said that whoever achieves something aspires to more and more instead of enjoying that triumph. I assure you that every day your life is full of small triumphs. Be thankful for them, share them, and enjoy them.

Life is wonderful and everything is going to work out in the end!

Steven

Wellbeing is far more than the absence of illness, pain, and disease.

Wellbeing incorporates our mental, emotional, physical, and spiritual health. This holistic approach to wellness produces greater levels of happiness, contentedness, energy, and exuberance.

My thinking about wellness changed when I came to understand that medicine in not healthcare. Food is healthcare. Exercise is healthcare. Meditation and mindfulness are healthcare. Afternoon naps are healthcare. Medicine is sick care!

It is health — in terms of overall wellbeing — that is true wealth. It's not the size of your house, the number of cars you own, or the digits in your bank account. Every day I paraphrase an Irish Proverb and tell myself, "No time for my wellbeing today, no wellbeing for my time tomorrow."

Be happy in the moment, that's enough.
Each moment is all we need, not more.

Mother Teresa

Wellbeing Quotes

Have regular hours for work and play; make each day both useful and pleasant, and prove that you understand the worth of time by employing it well. Then youth will be delightful, old age will bring few regrets and life will become a beautiful success.
Louisa May Alcott

Stress is an ignorant state. It believes that everything is an emergency. Nothing is that important.
Natalie Goldberg

No matter how much pressure you feel at work, if you could find ways to relax for at least five minutes every hour, you'd be more productive.
Dr. Joyce Brothers

Surviving is important, but thriving is elegant.
Maya Angelou

The most important thing I have learned over the years is the difference between taking one's work seriously and taking one's self seriously. The first is imperative, and the second disastrous.
Margaret Fonteyn

Solitude is such a potential thing. We hear voices in solitude, we never hear in the hurry and turmoil of life; we receive counsels and comforts, we get under no other condition.
Amelia Barr

The soul always knows how to heal itself. The challenge is to silence the mind.
Caroline Myss

How much bondage and suffering a woman escapes when she takes the liberty of being her own physician of both body and soul.
Elizabeth Cady Stanton

The universe is always speaking to us...sending us little messages, causing coincidences and serendipities, reminding us to stop, to look around, to believe in something else, something more.
Nancy Thayer

Happiness is good health and a bad memory.
Ingrid Bergman

Throw out an alarming alarm clock. If the ring is loud and strident, you're waking up to instant stress. You shouldn't be bullied out of bed, just reminded that it's time to start your day.
Sharon Gold

We cannot always control our thoughts, but we can control our words, and repetition impresses the subconscious, and we are then master of the situation.
Jane Fonda

The soul always knows what to do to heal itself. The challenge is to silence the mind.
Caroline Myss

As I see it every day you do one of two things: build health or produce disease in yourself.
Adelle Davis

Once you become consciously aware of just how powerful your thoughts are, you will realize everything in your life is exactly how you allow it to be.
Melanie Moushigian Koulouris

If worry were an effective weight-loss program, women would be invisible.
Nancy Drew

Break the anger habit. It is a waste of valuable energy to rail against adverse events. Stuff happens. Get over it and move on.
Sibyl McLendon

Laughter is the jam on the toast of life. It adds flavor, keeps it from being too dry and makes it easier to swallow.
Diane Johnson

Better by far you should forget and smile than you should remember and be sad.
Christina Rossetti

There is a way that nature speaks, that land speaks. Most of the time we are simply not patient enough, quiet enough, to pay attention to the story.
Linda Hogan

It is a wholesome and necessary thing for us to turn again to the earth and in the contemplation of her beauties to know the sense of wonder and humility.
Rachel Carson

A balanced life is hard to achieve in a world where success, power and physical appearance are thought of as so important.
Melissa Perry Moraja

Anxiety checks learning. A feeling of well-being and respect stimulates an alert mind.
Eda LeShan

Worry does not empty tomorrow of its sorrow, it empties today of its strength.
Corrie ten Boom

Nothing contributes so much to tranquilize the mind as a steady purpose — a point on which the soul may fix its intellectual eye.
Mary Wollstonecraft Shelley

If the sight of the blue skies fills you with joy, if a blade of grass springing up in the fields has power to move you, if the simple things in nature have a message you understand, rejoice, for your soul is alive.
Eleonora Duse

Thousands upon thousands of persons of have studied disease. Almost no one has studied health.
Adelle Davis

The thing that is really hard, and really amazing, is giving up on being perfect and beginning the work of becoming yourself.
Anna Quindlen

Be happy in the moment, that's enough. Each moment is all we need, not more.
Mother Teresa

Exercise is actually a great productivity tool for me. Productivity is more than just tackling the work that's in front of you. It's ensuring that you're fueled and inspired to get things done the best they possibly can be.
Jessica Alba

Every day brings a choice: to practice stress or peace.
Joan Borysenko

Breathe. Let go. And remind yourself that this very moment is the only one you know you have for sure.
Oprah Winfrey

Mindfulness isn't difficult, we just need to remember to do it.
Sharon Salzberg

Being a healthy woman isn't about getting on a scale or measuring your waistline. We need to start focusing on what matters — on how we feel, and how we feel about ourselves.
Michelle Obama

Relaxing in the midst of chaos, learning not to panic — this is the spiritual path.
Pema Chödrön

It is when the discomfort strikes that they realize a strong mind is the most powerful weapon of all.
Chrissie Wellington

Breathe. Let go. And remind yourself that this very moment is the only one you know you have for sure.
Oprah Winfrey

I am convinced that there are times in everybody's experience when there is so much to be done, that the only way to do it is to sit down and do nothing.
Fanny Fern

Never get so busy making a living that you forget to make a life.
Dolly Parton

Burnout is about resentment. Preventing it is about knowing yourself well enough to know what it is you're giving up; that makes you resentful.
Marissa Meyer

It stands to reason that anyone who learns to live well will die well. The skills are the same: being present in the moment, and humble, and brave, and keeping a sense of humor.
Victoria Moran

As long as we have practiced neither concentration nor mindfulness, the ego takes itself for granted and remains its usual normal size, as big as the people around one will allow.
Ayya Khema

Restore your attention or bring it to a new level by dramatically slowing down whatever you're doing.
Sharon Salzberg

I'm now ferociously healthy in body and mind. You couldn't pay me to go near a psychiatrist again. Stopping seeing them was my first step to getting well.
Margot Kidder

For fast-acting relief, try slowing down.
Lily Tomlin

Being healthy is more than just a number on the scale or the number from a test. These numbers are simply a moment in time.
Sharan Tash

The day she let go of the things that were weighing her down, was the day she began to shine the brightest.
Katrina Mayer

I always had the uncomfortable feeling that if I wasn't sitting in front of a computer typing, I was wasting my time — but I pushed myself to take a wider view of what was "productive." Time spent with my family and friends was never wasted.
Gretchen Rubin

Good health is not something we can buy. However, it can be an extremely valuable savings account.
Anne Wilson Schaef

Living in the moment brings you a sense of reverence for all of life's blessings.
Oprah Winfrey

A picnic is more than eating a meal, it is a pleasurable state of mind.
Dee Dee Stovel

Mindfulness meditation doesn't change life. Life remains as fragile and unpredictable as ever. Meditation changes the heart's capacity to accept life as it is.
Sylvia Boerstein

Those who contemplate the beauty of the Earth find reserves of strength that will endure as long as life lasts. There is symbolic as well as actual beauty in the migration of the birds, the ebb and flow of the tides, the folded bud ready for spring. There is something infinitely healing in the repeated refrains of nature — the assurance that dawn comes after night, and spring after the winter.
Rachel Carson

Mindfulness is all about managing stress in your internal world, regardless of what comes at you externally.
Michelle Kinder

You must learn to be still in the midst of activity and to be vibrantly alive in repose.
Indira Gandhi

All the money in the world can't buy you back good health.
Reba McEntire

Once you have a major success with assertiveness, you learn that it's a much healthier path than being a doormat to the insensitive folks. You gain respect for yourself, have more time for your priorities, and develop authentic and healthier relationships.
Doreen Virtue

If you seek peace, be still. If you seek wisdom, be silent. If you seek love, be yourself.
Becca Lee

Balance suggests a perfect equilibrium. There is no such thing. That is a false expectation. There are going to be priorities and dimensions of your life; how you integrate them is how you find true happiness.
Denise Morrison

Everyone must take time to sit and watch the leaves turn.
Elizabeth Lawrence

My number one daily habit is to give myself permission to be happy. It's physical and mental; it's my diet, physical activity, and emotional state. That's all tied together.
Michelle Obama

A balanced life is hard to achieve in a world where success, power and physical appearance are thought of as so important.
Melissa Perry Moraja

In order to experience everyday spirituality, we need to remember that we are spiritual beings spending some time in a human body.
Barbara De Angelis

You simply will not be the same person two months from now after consciously giving thanks each day for the abundance that exists in your life. And you will have set in motion an ancient spiritual law: the more you have and are grateful for, the more will be given you.
Sarah Ban Breathnach

Breathe. Let go. And remind yourself that this very moment is the only one you know you have for sure.
Oprah Winfrey

When we go back in to the past and rake up all the troubles we've had, we end up reeling and staggering through life. Stability and peace of mind come by living in the moment.
Pam W. Vredevelt

Be present. I would encourage you with all my heart just to be present. Be present and open to the moment that is unfolding before you. Because, ultimately, your life is made up of moments. So, don't miss them by being lost in the past or anticipating the future.
Jessica Lange

One of the most courageous decisions you'll ever make is to finally let go of whatever is hurting your heart and soul.
Brigitte Nicole

You don't always need a plan. Sometimes you just need to breathe, trust, let go and see what happens.
Mandy Hale

Almost everything will work again if you unplug it for a few minutes...including you.
Anne Lamott

Staying in the present will keep you grounded and engaged.
Karen R. Koenig

Happiness is the consequence of personal effort.
Elizabeth Gilbert

Balance is not better time management, but better boundary management. Balance means making choices and enjoying those choices.
Betsy Jacobson

Special Acknowledgement

My dear Berenice.

From the bottom of my heart, I thank you for the beautiful project we did with this trilogy of books focused on the entrepreneurial woman who wants to improve herself and give the best version of herself as a professional, mother, wife, daughter, friend and professional.

This journey that we began last year, where it was first a dream and then, with all the dedication, work, love, and passion that we both put into this project, became a reality where together we have touched or at least sensitized the lives of many women.

Thank you, my friend, for your dedication, hours of work, for always giving your best and fulfilling the times that Steven and I asked of you despite having other works of art to work on and complete.

I am convinced that these books brought us closer together and gave us the opportunity to share the best of ourselves. For this and many other reasons, I admire you a lot. I admire you as a professional, as a mother, wife, daughter, sister, and friend.

I take this beautiful experience with me, hoping that we will continue to travel together on the path of life and that, as women fighters, we will always continue to support each other.

With love,
Adriana

About the Authors

Adriana Fuentes Díaz is the author of the award-winning book *When Strong Women Speak, Strong Women Listen* and *Strong Women Have Beliefs and Values*.

She was born in Mexico City, spent most of her childhood and early adult years in Venezuela, and returned to her city of birth seven years ago. She also lived in Newark, Delaware for a year as high school Exchange Student with a wonderful family.

After graduating with a degree in Communication and Advertising in Venezuela, Adriana studied Public Relations at McGill University in Montreal, Canada. This led to a 15-year career in marketing, communications, and public relations across a wide range of industries, including oil &

gas, automotive, entertainment, beauty and skincare products, and financial services.

Passionate about branding, she is the recipient of three prestigious Advertising Industry Awards for her work on television commercials for the Mercedes-Benz brand in Mexico, including a Cannes Bronze Lion, an Ojo de Iberoamérica, and an A&AD (Global Association for Creative Advertising & Design). She also promotes her passion for branding with talks on luxury brands and marketing at the Universidad Iberoamericana in Mexico City.

While at the BBDO advertising company in Mexico City, Adriana was the leader of the BBDO Inspira program where she delivered workshops for women staff in search of personal and professional balance. In addition, she has been a volunteer and a supporter of programs and organizations of women entrepreneurs to foster gender equality in the professions and workplace.

A deeply committed dog lover for many years, Adriana created Gente Zoo, a foundation in Venezuela for stray animals on the streets, which is supported by a wide range of professionals.

Besides her devotion to her teenage son, her hobbies include traveling, reading, exercising outdoors, and sharing meals with family and friends.

Steven Howard is an award-winning author of 22 leadership, business, and motivational books. When he is not writing he specializes in creating and delivering Leadership Development programs for frontline leaders, mid-level leaders, supervisors, senior leaders, and high-potential leaders.

Steven has over 40 years of international senior sales, marketing, and leadership experience. His corporate career covered a wide variety of fields and experiences, including Regional Marketing Director for Texas Instruments Asia-Pacific, Regional Director (South Asian & ASEAN) for TIME Magazine, Global Account Director at BBDO Advertising handling an international airline account, and Vice President Marketing for Citibank's Consumer Banking Group.

Steven is the author of 22 leadership, marketing, and management books and the editor of nine professional and personal development books in the *Project You* series.

His other books are:

Coaching Words of Wisdom: Quotes from the World of Sports to Help You Be Better in Business and Life

How Stress and Anxiety Impact Your Decision Making

Better Decisions Better Thinking Better Outcomes: How to go from Mind Full to Mindful Leadership

8 Keys to Becoming a Great Leader: With leadership lessons and tips from Gibbs, Yoda & Capt'n Jack Sparrow

Leadership Lessons from the Volkswagen Saga

Asian Words of Success

Indispensable Asian Words of Knowledge

Asian Words of Inspiration

Asian Words of Meaning

The Book of Asian Proverbs

Marketing Words of Wisdom

The Best of the Monday Morning Marketing Memo

Powerful Marketing Memos

Corporate Image Management: A Marketing Discipline

Powerful Marketing Minutes: 50 Ways to Develop Market Leadership

MORE Powerful Marketing Minutes: 50 New Ways to Develop Market Leadership

Asian Words of Wisdom

Asian Words of Knowledge

Essential Asian Words of Wisdom

Pillars of Growth: Strategies for Leading Sustainable Growth (co-author with three others)

Motivation Plus Marketing Equals Money (co-author with four others)

www.ingramcontent.com/pod-product-compliance
Lightning Source LLC
Chambersburg PA
CBHW032059080426
42733CB00006B/346